FRONT PORCH SKETCHES

Stories from Cyrus Creek
When Times Were simple

BRENDA BOND

iUniverse, Inc.
Bloomington

Front Porch Sketches
Stories from Cyrus Creek When Times Were Simple

Cover painting and interior sketches by Brenda Bond

iUniverse books may be ordered through booksellers or by contacting:

iUniverse
1663 Liberty Drive
Bloomington, IN 47403
www.iuniverse.com
1-800-Authors (1-800-288-4677)

ISBN: 978-1-4759-3347-5 (sc)
ISBN: 978-1-4759-3348-2 (e)
ISBN: 978-1-4759-3349-9 (dj)

Library of Congress Control Number: 2012910779

Printed in the United States of America

iUniverse rev. date: 7/26/2012

Dedication

This book is dedicated to the memory of the good people of the Cyrus Creek community who are now departed, but not forgotten, and to the few remaining who have spent their lives here.

It is also dedicated to Cela Jo, daughter of my dear late sister, Dova; to my husband Jim; my sister Rosa; my granddaughter Dhania; and son and daughter, JB and Andrea Beth. I hope they relive a little of their Pa-paw and Ma-maw "Tootle's" way of life through this book.

Acknowledgements

I want to thank Dr. John Patrick Grace for his work and his encouragement in my Life Writing Class.

Thank you to my fellow classmate writers. Your words meant so much and kept me writing until the completion of this book.

Table of Contents

Preface

When I signed up to take a writing class from Dr. John Patrick Grace, I knew I wanted to write about life as it used to be when I was a child. Now, life seems complicated and fast-paced. Back then, our way of life was simple as Kool-Aid. Families stuck together like burrs on a dog. With this thought in mind, I began writing. It seemed the more I wrote, the more I could remember.

I had a good childhood, and it was so pleasant to relive it as I wrote. My parents were good people who took me to church and they probably spoiled me a bit too much. Our community was small, and many people had their grade school education at Watson Elementary through the years. So many, in fact, that there is an annual reunion for all those former Watson students. They gather each year in August to renew old friendships and talk about "old times."

As I thought, I wrote, and wrote, and wrote. Finally, I had completed my book by the end of the Life Writing Class.

Introduction

While writing my story, so many people and events of everyday life went through my mind. I hope you will relive life with me as it was in the fifties; so simple, mostly happy, and family and community oriented. I know that I was fortunate to have been born into a good family. I had no doubts that I was loved. My oldest sister was very special, and I want my niece to know the important place that her mother held in my life as a child, and why my heart could never forget her.

I want my children to stay in touch with who they are and their family heritage. The things that are most important in life cannot be bought, but can be learned and passed on through the way our families lived. Honesty, hard work, and plain old common sense, were things my parents practiced throughout their lives. Their spiritual lives were the very core of their being, for what is life without belief in a Creator, who put everything on this earth for a reason? We all take things for granted—that is human. We look, but often do not see that what is right before us is a gift from God.

Go with me as I travel through my childhood. I have tried to put things in order as much as possible in my book, especially the school years. I did not write a lot about my children. That would be another generation and I wanted to concentrate on the fifties and early sixties.

I can still see our colorful yard that held many varieties of flowers that my mother loved so much, and my dad complaining every time he mowed and had to be careful not to cut any of them down. I can see our little house after Daddy painted it an aqua color when colorful houses were in style. I remember the smell of sassafras tea as it simmered on the stovetop on a cold winter day.

I can remember sitting in church and hearing the hard shelled bugs beating against the screens on the open windows, as my mother entertained me by folding her fancy handkerchief into twin babies in a cradle.

Cyrus Creek, of Barboursville, West Virginia, is where my maternal grandparents set up their household and raised their family. My mother, her sister and a brother remained on Cyrus Creek, where they raised *their* families. I experienced the joy of growing up with my first cousins and we had such fun together. We jumped rope, played games, made playhouses and played with our dolls. We sometimes played movie star, and dressed up in old dresses and high heels (I was always Marilyn Monroe). We caught lightning bugs, played in the creek and climbed the hill behind and in front of my home. There were few cars and we could safely ride our bikes on the road. We had no computers or technical gadgets like children today, but we were happy. When no children were around to play with, I entertained myself by drawing, coloring, or reading. I cannot remember being bored. Children in the fifties remained children much longer than they do now.

Church was the center of our community. There was always something going on there. There was the annual *homecoming* where people came back to enjoy a dinner set out on long picnic tables outside. The food was plentiful, with every kind of food you could imagine. My grandmother Scarberry was known for her "burnt sugar cake" and everyone tried to get a piece before it was all gone. There was gospel music nearly all day at the homecoming. Sometimes in the summer, there was a tent revival and a large tent was set up, usually in Chapman's field. It would go on for a week. People went to church Sunday morning, then again in the evening. There was church on Wednesday evenings as well.

Growing up in the country encouraged love of family and friends, respect for God and compassion for the animals and wildlife He has given us. The country was a good place to live. There is an old saying, "You can never go home again." But I have gone home again, not once, but twice, as you will read. I know my parents and grandparents would approve of our "homecoming."

Cyrus Creek Community

Cyrus Creek is just east of the Huntington Mall in West Virginia. After driving over the new bridge, there is a traffic light. To the right is Cyrus Creek Road. It is a creek valley that lies between various sized hills. The old Watson Elementary School is gone. In its place is a business called *Tungston Nippon USA.* To the right is a new entrance road to East Trails End. Above that level, even with the road is another new business: *Dog House Motorsports.*

The creek meanders crookedly up the road. In some places it is in front of houses. Those houses have bridges to cross. The creek ran behind our house. I have not seen the creek out of its banks often; it usually just comes up level with the bank during hard summer storms, then drops quickly when the rain stops. Many years before I was born, the creek flooded and water came up under the house. My mother always had a fear that it would happen again.

I have always assumed that Cyrus Creek was named after the many Cyrus families who lived here. Most of them have lived their lives and gone on, with very few of their descendants still living on Cyrus Creek.

In my community of Cyrus Creek, I never considered us poor. We had as much as our neighbors. I never had "hand-me-down-clothes" because my half-sisters were so much older. Mother always bought new clothes for me. Many came from *Huntington Dry Goods,* later called *The Huntington Store* and many were ordered from *Aldens* catalog. Sometimes I was allowed to select my Easter dress or another special occasion dress from this catalog. Mother ordered other items as well. Anticipation was the best part of a catalog order. Every day I would wait for the mailman to come, and finally one day he would reach behind his seat and hand me a large bundle, wrapped in brown paper and tied with string. What joy!

We had plenty of food, and meals consisted of plain country cooking. People did not often eat out in my community as they do now. There were no fast food restaurants.

Movies were a rare treat. My first experience with a movie was not good. I was about four when Mother took me to see a Roy Rogers movie at the little theater in Barboursville. There was a scene where a mountain lion jumped onto Trigger's back (Roy's horse) and viciously attacked. There was much noise from both animals. It scared me to death and I started crying and screaming. It looked so real! Mother had to take me out into the lobby until I quieted down and the mountain lion was gone.

Most people on Cyrus Creek found their contentment visiting relatives and neighbors, sitting on the front porch and just talking. Occasionally we made a trip to Huntington to shop. We dressed in our good clothes. People were not as casual in their dress as they are now. The *fifties* was a conservative decade.

Church History

In 1922, the old school building one mile up the road on Cyrus Creek was purchased from the Cabell County Board of Education. It had served as a school for many years, and now it became a church: *Cyrus Creek Holiness Mission.* The name was later changed to *Cyrus Creek Missionary Baptist Church,* in 1956.

This old church was eventually demolished and replaced by a much larger brick facility. In 1970 it was dedicated, and it still stands and is used today. When the old church was being torn down, it was first emptied. There was an old library-style desk with two drawers and a chair. My mother was the only one who knew the history behind it, as she had attended this school through eighth grade, and this desk was used by her teachers. She told me one of her male teachers used to stand her on top of the desk and ask her to recite poems. She was a good student and they did a lot of memorization in her school days. The workers gave my mother the desk and chair, and she gave them to me. I stripped the many layers of tan paint away and it was a beautiful golden oak wood. There were several circles burned into the surface of the desk. Mother said they were from the burners on the stove that heated the room. I left those historical circles on the desk and did not try to sand them off, as they were a part of its history. I still have the old desk and use it almost daily.

Family Sketches

My parents were *old.* At least they were to my mind and indeed, when I was growing up, parents were much younger. My cousins and playmates had young parents. My mother, Gladys Peyton Edwards, was thirty-eight years old and my father, Walter Edwards, was forty years when I was born. It was a second marriage for both. My dad had a daughter and was a widower. Mother had two daughters and was a widow. Mother's first husband died of a ruptured appendix. Peritonitis set in and penicillin had not yet been discovered. He died from infection. Daddy's first wife died from tuberculosis.

Samuel Peyton, Mother's first husband, had purchased three lots up the road from the little house they rented on Cyrus Creek. He had never had the time or the money to build a home. After his death Mother's uncle, Arch Smith, and neighbors went together and built a small frame house for her and the girls. That was typical of how neighbors looked after and helped each other then.

When I was old enough to understand, Mother told me how hard it was to survive during the Depression without a husband to help. She said, "Brennie, there was hardly any money to put food on the table and care for two little girls. I didn't even have a dollar to buy stockings to wear to church."

After meeting at the Cyrus Creek church, my parents were eventually married. They had a family of three children between them, and planned no more. Surprise—I came along four years later.

Mother's daughter, Dova, or "Dodie" as I called her, was seventeen years old when I was born. Daddy's daughter, Emalene, was fourteen. She eloped at sixteen and left, so I have no memories of her at home. Phyllis, Mother's other daughter, was nine. Dodie is the one I remember best. She apparently doted on me and became my personal babysitter, or second mother.

Mother and Daddy took me to church with them from the time I was born. I can vaguely remember, at age two, being in the *card class.* It was taught by Eva Paul, and later, it was taught by Idella Thomas, also known as Dot.

In Sunday school, we sang *This Little Light of Mine, Jesus Loves Me, I've Got the Joy, Joy, Joy* and others. We listened to stories about people in the Bible: David and Goliath, Samson, Daniel, Jonah, Joseph, and my favorite, Noah's Ark. I always wondered why God wanted snakes on the ark. To my way of thinking, He should have let them drown in the flood! Dot always asked us questions after the stories. There was usually only one boy, Gary, who answered them all. We all thought he was very smart. Dot's nephews were in the class. One of them always tried her patience. He made a loud "pop" by putting his finger in his mouth, and causing the "pop" by the way he brought it out. It sounded just like a cork being pulled out of a bottle. She threatened him every week, but it did no good.

I never missed a Sunday. Every year I received a number to go in my attendance pin, which was the number of years I attended without missing. It stopped at eleven years.

Sunday

My parents, being devout Baptists, believed in keeping the Sabbath. They did no work or as little as possible on Sunday, for it was a day of rest, devoted to the Lord and worship. Daddy never mowed the yard or worked in the garden, or anything he could do on other days of the week. On Saturdays, Mother did as much of the cooking as possible and put it away for Sunday dinner. She usually baked a cake or made pies as well.

After breakfast on Sunday morning, we dressed in our Sunday best. This meant Daddy wore a suit and tie, Mother wore a pretty floral dress and hose that ended at her knees, and sometimes a little hat and white gloves. I always had several pretty dresses, so I wore one of those with my suede shoes in the winter, and white sandals in the summer. We walked the few yards up the road to the church.

Lewis Brillie Scarberry (my maternal grandfather) started church by ringing a bell to get everyone quiet. The congregation would read the responses as he read the lesson from the quarterly. The choir would sing a song. Then my grandfather announced: "The Sunday schools will now arrange themselves; teachers take charge of the classes." We would all go to our rooms or sections of the church where Sunday school was held. Afterward, there would be the secretary's report and more singing. Then there would be preaching for at least an hour—often longer.

I was always small and a picky eater. Mother prepared hearty country meals through the week. Daddy worked for the C & O railroad and came home hungry every evening. She cooked tomato dumplings, fried turnips, stewed potatoes, pinto beans and cornbread, and kale. We did not always eat meat. If we did, it would be in a meatloaf or maybe pork chops. These meals never appealed to me. As I was a bit spoiled and so small for my age, Mother would humor me by heating up a can of Campbell's alphabet soup. I have often said that were it not for the Campbell's soup, I would have starved to death!

On Sunday, however, our dinner was a feast of foods I truly loved. We had wonderful crispy fried chicken and mashed potatoes, or sometimes it might be a roast with carrots and onions cooked together. We had fresh vegetables from the garden in the summer and the half-runner green beans were the best! People from other areas often steam green beans with almond slivers or make them into casseroles. Rural West Virginians know the best way is to cook them on the stovetop for an hour to an hour and a half; season with a strip or two of bacon or ham, a chunk of onion, and a bit of salt and pepper. Mother added a tablespoon of butter when done. You eat the beans with sliced red tomatoes, green onions, and bell peppers. Yum!

Mother left most leftover food on top of the kitchen stove, except for foods like potato salad or coleslaw. She covered everything until time to eat again that evening. We never got food poisoning from this habit.

Daddy never forgot to say the blessing before our meals. He called it "returning thanks." It was nearly always the same prayer in all the years that I lived at home.

Many times through the years, someone would knock on our front door just as we sat down for dinner. It was usually one of Daddy's three brothers. Company was always welcomed and a place was set at the table for the visitor (it was country custom to do so). I was very shy around people I did not see often, and hated to eat in front of them, so I ate very little and left the table as soon as I was allowed.

Daddy's brothers usually ignored me, except for Uncle Clarence. He was always trying to make up with me, but being shy, I seldom answered him. One Sunday, Uncle Clarence was carrying a bag, and he handed it to me. "Bonnie sent this to you." Bonnie was his youngest daughter. I opened it and it was a little red plaid skirt with pleats. Mother had to prompt me to say, "Thank you." I was thrilled to wear this pretty little skirt, my first of only two hand-me-downs in my life! From then on, I liked Uncle Clarence best of all of Daddy's brothers.

As an adult, I have belonged to two other Christian denominations. Keeping the Sabbath day holy was not emphasized nor often practiced at either church. I have come to the conclusion that we each do what is right in our hearts as much as possible and I keep the Sabbath as I was raised.

Springtime

Spring is so beautiful in West Virginia. The dogwood and redbud trees paint our hills with such lovely grandeur. Forsythia is usually the first sign that spring is on the way, followed by crocuses, grape hyacinths, jonquils and tulips. I can still picture my mother's yard ablaze with patches of color. Pansies were her favorite. Mother worried each spring when her crocuses bloomed that they would get their little heads frozen, and sometimes they did. One time, near Easter, Mother came home to find one of her young trees was growing colorful Easter eggs. Easter bunny, Dova, had been there!

Easter was a time my family looked forward to. It was springtime and a time of rebirth—new flowers, new leaves on trees, new baby birds and animals. It also brought me a basket each Easter morning, delivered by the Easter bunny, of course.

We bought new Easter outfits which we wore to church on Sunday. Nearly every lady and little girl wore a new bonnet or hat and white gloves. My little dress was always fancy and in a pretty pastel color for spring. I knew why we celebrated Easter. As a child, Good Friday was usually a cloudy, gray day with no sun. I actually could picture Jesus hanging on the cross. It was so sad to die in such a cruel way. Easter Sunday was a joyous time to celebrate His resurrection.

Children all looked forward to hiding Easter eggs. They were not plastic eggs made in China, like they use today, but real hen eggs that were boiled. Coloring them with dyes was almost as much fun as hiding them. We wrote on them with a wax pencil and put stamps on them, and anything to make them decorative. We had an egg hunt at Watson Elementary each year. We each brought six colored eggs to hide. Sometimes our Sunday school class would meet on Sunday afternoon for the hunt. There was usually a prize egg and the child who found this won a chocolate Easter bunny or some kind of goody.

One Easter I particularly remember was when I was seven years old. I was hiding eggs with my cousins in our yard. It had just rained, so everything was still dripping wet. I was wearing my new white open-toed sandals. We were having so much fun, until I looked down and a long earthworm was hanging out of my shoe under the arch of my foot. Even then, I detested anything gross. I started screaming and kicked that shoe high in the air, worm and all! I hopped back to the house and Mother had to go and retrieve my shoe. I refused to wear it again until she had disinfected it and set it in the sun to dry.

When Jim (now my husband) and I began dating, we were driving on a country road in the springtime. Dogwood and redbud trees were in their glorious bloom. I told Jim how much I loved dogwood. He immediately stopped the car, got out and cut off several twigs of dogwood flowers with his pocket knife. He got back in the car and handed them to me. He said, "There's something wrong with these—they have bad places on the petals and I looked, but they're all the same." I thought he was kidding me, but I realized he was not. I said, "Jim, they're supposed to be like this. The four petals symbolize the cross. The bad places on each petal show the nails that were used to nail Jesus to the cross, and the center is the crown of thorns they placed on His head." Jim did not know this. I guess he never learned this in his church, or maybe he was not listening.

By Memorial Day, the early spring flowers were gone, but many other varieties were blooming. I helped cut flowers to put in jars of water to take to the cemetery. My parents bought wreaths to put on their former spouses' graves, but we used flowers from our yard to remember the rest of our departed ones.

Dodie taught me how to make roses from crepe paper. She cut up wire hangers for the stems and she had several pretty packages of crepe paper: red, pink, yellow, and green. After we attached the flower to the stem and wrapped it with strips of green, she heated up paraffin wax on the stove. Then we dipped the roses into it, coating and making them water-proof. I thought they were beautiful. We took these to the Blue Sulphur cemetery to decorate graves, as well.

Decoration Day, as we called Memorial Day, was a big deal. Not only was it a time to remember departed friends and relatives, but also to visit other living friends and relatives in the cemetery. Mother always bought me a pretty spring dress to wear, usually white. One I vividly remember choosing was a sleeveless seersucker dress with tiny aqua blue flowers on a white background. It had a fifty-yard skirt. It was fun to spin 'round and 'round, making the skirt flare out in a circle around me. I was told never to step on a grave. That would disrespect the dead. My mother and father would stand and visit in the cemetery forever, it seemed.

The Blue Sulphur Cemetery consists of two parts—the old cemetery, and the new. The old cemetery is behind the Mud River Baptist Church and the new part is to the right. The two areas are separated by a small stream.

Barboursville

Barboursville, West Virginia, is less than ten minutes from Cyrus Creek. Its boundaries have now reached beyond the Huntington Mall, but the town itself is what I am referring to. My family did most of their business in Barboursville. Dr. W.D. Bourn, our family doctor, had his office there, as did our dentist, Dr. Charles T. Withers. The banking was done at *First State Bank*. My family always used *Wallace Funeral Home* when there was a death. They were related to us on my grandmother Scarberry's side of the family.

The best thing in Barboursville when I was a child was *Shy's Ten Cent Store*, located on the corner of Central Avenue. They had everything. With a dime, you could buy a bag full of assorted candies. You could buy a little sparkling birthstone ring, doll clothes, and anything else you could think of. When my mother's birthday came around, I always begged Daddy to take me to the ten cent store so I could buy her a present. Her Mother's Day gift always came from the same store. Her present was once a blue rhinestone brooch. It was the prettiest thing I had ever seen and it cost a lot—one dollar! Other times it was a figurine of a dog, a pair of glass vases, or a box of fancy handkerchiefs. It always took a good while for me to decide, but I picked the best present, and was so proud to see Mother smile when she opened it.

The library was located on Main Street in a small white building. Mrs. Sue Alexander worked there as the librarian and also when the new brick library was built as well. Little did I know that I would eventually be employed there, starting in 1969.

Barboursville Junior High was on Main Street, where I attended school. Parts of it were pretty rickety even then. The old "B" building was first to be torn down. The location of the old school is now the beautiful *Nancy Cartmill Park,* named after the town mayor at the time. The *Village Inn* on the corner across from the school was the place to eat, if you did not like cafeteria food. The milkshakes were delicious. Barboursville High was on Central Avenue at the second viaduct. It was a two story building which later became the middle school. Even that is gone now. In its place is the new Barboursville Middle School.

There was a small department store called *Updyke's.* It was beside the ten cent store. Daddy bought me my first grown-up purse there (we called them pocket books). It was displayed in the window. The purse was black cloth with a gold fastener and a clear Lucite handle. *Brady's Hardware* had anything you can imagine. Daddy went there for tools, garden supplies, nails and screws, plumbing pipes, etc. It was our *Walmart* of that time.

My great-uncle, Herman Grove, lived in an attractive white house to the left after you went through the Barboursville tunnel from Route 60. The yard was outlined by perfectly trimmed hedges. He was the brother of my grandmother, Julia Edith Helen Grove Scarberry.

The Mud River used to get out of its bank and cover a portion of Route 60. The old bridge was usually flooded as well. It was replaced by the *William C. Turman Bridge*.

One thing that May brought each year (besides flowers) was the annual band festival in Huntington. High school bands from counties throughout West Virginia came to Huntington on school buses to participate in the marching parade. I was nearly always there. When the Barboursville High School Band marched by, we cheered loudly. It just seemed to me that they were always the best.

One year, I went to see the parade with my cousin. Her older sister, who was a student at Barboursville High, had painted a pirate on a bass drum (their mascot was the pirate). Donna was, and still is, an excellent artist and we watched with pride as her pirate art went by.

Usually, along the way, several band members would pass out from the heat. Even in May, it was often pretty warm. The band route varied through the years, but they nearly always marched down Fourth Avenue. There, in front of the WSAZ TV studio, they performed for the camera. Now, with the consolidation of so many high schools in the state, the annual band festival is only a happy memory from the past.

BARBOURSVILLE
PIRATES

Country Living

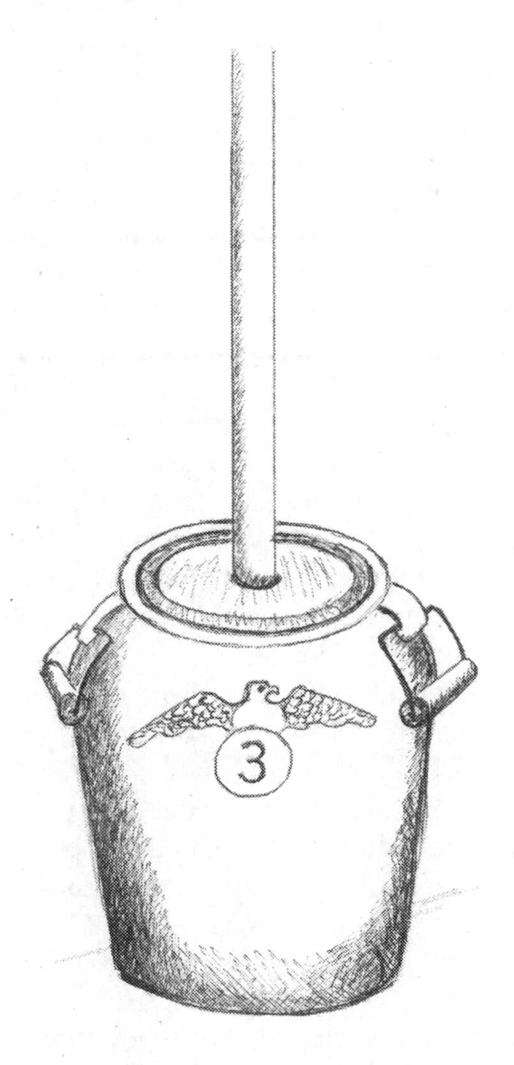

Pop Scarberry kept a stand of honey bees behind his house. We had to be careful not to get near them when playing, or angry bees would sting us. Pop put on his *beekeeper's garb,* which included a hat with netting that covered his face and neck, and a pair of gloves. He robbed the bees and put the honey in buckets. I liked chewing on the wax.

Mom Scarberry churned butter in a stoneware crock. When it was ready, she put it in a wooden mold that made a pretty design on top of the butter. Pop would bring us a mold of fresh butter, which I loved. My mother never ate it. She said she had had enough of cows when she had to do milking at home. Their tails would swish her in the face or they would step in the milk bucket. Suffice it to say, she had no love for cows or any of their products.

Summer was always a busy time for Mother. My dad planted a garden with tomatoes, green beans, corn, cucumbers, bell peppers, onions, potatoes, radishes, and carrots. He always burned a bed for lettuce. Mother canned all that she could for winter. But that was not all. We had a crabapple tree. It was always so heavy with apples that the branches had to be propped up with poles so they would not break. Those tiny apples made the best jelly. There were enough apples for all the neighbors who wanted them. Mother was always inviting neighbors, "Come and bring a basket with you."

My mother and father had a big copper kettle and they made apple butter in the fall for several years. They sat on the front porch and peeled what seemed like many bushels of apples. The neighbors or some of the family helped. It was a big job. Daddy bought an apple peeler that he thought would make it go faster. You stuck the apple on a spike and turned a handle. This would rotate the apple as the peeler took off the skin in long unbroken strands. After the apples were cooking in the big kettle, my dad would stir with a long handled wooden tool he had made. Mother added the sugar as well as the oil of cinnamon. She liked lots of cinnamon. I once begged her for the empty cinnamon bottle. She told me to be careful with it. Being quite young, I didn't know that it would burn if it got on your skin. Somehow I got it on my neck and it made big red splotches that burned like fire.

When the apple butter was thick and ready, the waiting jars were filled and sealed. We had homemade biscuits with apple butter all winter.

Whenever there was fruit to be canned, the peeling took place on the front porch. My favorite time was when Mother canned peaches. I always hung around, getting my fill of the sweet, fresh fruit. Stringing beans was always done on the porch as well. Daddy could string twice as many beans as anyone else.

My grandparents had wild plum trees on their property. I can remember picking plums with my cousins and putting all I could hold in my pockets. We went back down to the old well and pumped fresh cold water over them before eating. These plums were much smaller than the domesticated variety you buy in the stores, but very sweet.

Country living was not all about food. My father could play a banjo. I remember Daddy playing *Cripple Creek, Turkey in the Straw,* and *Old Man Tucker.* Daddy could make a puzzle with wire, bending it into a "U" shape with a bar across the top. A heart hung on the bar with no opening in it. To solve it, you had to figure out how to remove the heart. From a small branch, Daddy could also make a neat whistle that made a loud shrill noise. Kids were always begging him to make a whistle and he would whip out his pocket knife and find a hickory tree, cut off a slim branch, and begin carving. He was always sitting around *whittling* with his knife.

My father could also make his shoes last a long time. He had a cobbler's shoe and anvil that he used to half-sole his shoes. He would often put taps on the heels of my shoes. I thought they made wonderful tap-dancing shoes and I tapped all over the place with them.

In our backyard there was a walnut tree just right for a swing. Daddy put up a rope swing for me. I could sing and swing forever, it seemed. My favorite songs to sing were *Santa Lucia,* and *Sweet and Low.* We sang both these songs in school. I also hummed the theme from *Dragnet,* a popular TV police show, over and over.

My dad was never still for long—nervous energy, I guess. Every spring, he set the porch chairs out in the yard and gave them a fresh coat of paint. He cleaned the gutters and every other year, gave the house a new coat of paint.

One summer, my sister Emalene's husband, Acie, was helping Daddy with some work on the roof. They were in and out dozens of times, and in the attic. Mother was preparing dinner at noontime and had started dishing it up and putting it on the table. Suddenly, without warning, my brother-in-law came crashing through the ceiling, landing right in the middle of the kitchen table on the food! What a mess!

We had a telephone, but in the rural areas, we had to share lines. This was called a *party line.* Ours was shared by two other families. We each had a code ring. Our ring was a long and two shorts. It was pretty common for people to listen in or eavesdrop on another's conversation, but you could usually tell when someone lifted the receiver. When I was in my teens and received daily evening calls from a boyfriend, one older lady apparently did not like this form of *courting* on the phone. She would butt in and ask to use the phone because she had to call the doctor. Being polite, I always told her "all right," said goodbye to my boyfriend, and hung up. She sure did have to call that doctor an unusual number of times every week!

The milk truck ran every week on Cyrus Creek. We bought our bottled milk from Bordens. I drank lots of milk, and for a treat I could sometimes have the milkman deliver a quart of chocolate milk. People washed the bottles and put them out for the milkman to pick up each week. He seemed to know what each family ordered. If you wanted something different or needed extra, there was a cardboard selector. Just put up the brown flag and stick the cardboard selector into the top of the bottle and the milkman knew to leave chocolate milk, or buttermilk or other dairy products. The bottled milk had a cardboard stopper with a tab you pulled to open the glass bottle. On the underside of the cardboard, it was coated with thick cream, which I loved to lick.

My parents never financed a new piece of furniture nor an appliance that I know of. They simply waited until they had saved enough money to pay for it. I think we appreciated things more when we had to wait for them, and I was taught to take care of our furnishings and my own things. I remember three of my uncles who built their houses in stages. They paid for the materials to get the house under roof and do wiring and plumbing. Then they moved the family in and continued working to finish the house as they had the money for each step. It often took several years, but by the time it was completed, it was paid in full.

My dad bought used cars because he could pay cash for them, but he did not have enough money for a brand new car. Actually, the very last car he bought was new; a Plymouth Duster. He could not pay cash for a Cadillac, but he could pay cash for a Plymouth, so that is what he bought. Country people lived that way. *There is much to be said about living within your income, and nothing wrong with saying "I can't afford it."*

Wash Day

My mother was typical of the way women worked in the early fifties. Monday was *wash* day. It took a whole day to do the laundry in the Maytag wringer washer. It had to be filled manually with buckets of water from the faucet. A table on the left held a galvanized wash tub which was filled with rinse water. After agitating each load for a period of time, the washer was stopped by pulling out a knob and each piece of clothing was put between the wringer rolls, pressing out the soapy water and put into the rinse tub. Then each piece was put through the wringer again, getting out excess water. For white clothes, Mother used *bluing* in the rinse water. It was a small bottle and sprinkled in for the desired amount. She also had a bucket with Argo starch in the water. She dipped clothes in this and ran them through the wringer. Spray starch had not yet been invented.

The job of hanging the clothes on the line came next. Mother took a rag and wiped the metal clothesline to get the black off. Clothes were hung in a certain way and everything was grouped: sheets and pillow cases, socks, dresses, pants, etc. By evening, everything was dry and clothes were taken down and folded, or sprinkled with water if they were starched, and bundled in a basket for ironing the next day. If a sudden rain blew up, it was panic time to take the clothes down before they got wet again.

It would be a hardship to go back to this method of drying clothes, but my laundry never comes out of the dryer smelling like sunshine, the way my mother's used to.

Ironing Day

Tuesdays were for ironing the previous day's wash. Mother had an older friend and neighbor, Lizzie, who came up on Tuesdays and spent the day crocheting while she ironed in the kitchen. Lizzie always smelled like sweet shrubs. This is a fragrant small flower bud that blooms on a bush. I always referred to her as Mrs. Chapman. Children back then did not call adults by their first names. That was disrespectful.

I was allowed to sit in a corner and color or play with my dolls, but I was always listening. Being a quiet child, I never talked or interrupted. Sometimes, if they talked about something I should not listen to, one of them would nod at me and say, "Little pitchers have big ears," and the subject was quickly changed.

Mrs. Chapman crocheted beautiful doilies, pillowcases, and borders around handkerchiefs. She also made quilts, totally by hand. For my tenth birthday, she gave me a beautiful pink, double wedding ring design quilt. The stitches were tiny and perfect. *Occasionally, I like to get out the crocheted pillowcases and quilt and use them in my guest room, remembering Mrs. Chapman. I will always keep them.*

I was in the seventh grade when I got on the school bus one morning. Cousin Kathy asked, "Did you hear about Mrs. Chapman?" I replied, "No, what about her?" "She died last night," my cousin told me. The rest of the day I thought about her. She was quite old, and it was apparently her time, but I sure would miss her.

As a child, I never really had many responsibilities at home. When I was old enough, Mother gave me the job of washing her canning jars while she prepared the food that was to be preserved. Jars were stored in cardboard boxes in the outbuilding where she did the washing, so they had dust and a few dead bugs in them.

I sometimes followed my mother along and handed her clothespins as she hung each piece of laundry on the line. When I was tall enough, I wiped the clothesline clean before she began hanging them.

Dusting the living room tables and *what-nots* became my job because it was the one thing my mother hated to do. She had so many other chores to do that she didn't have the patience, I guess. Many households in the fifties had figurines that required frequent dusting.

From age twelve, I cleaned my own room. Not only did I make my bed and dust, I took everything off the floor and ran the dust mop, then mopped the floor in pine cleaner. I loved having my room neat and clean. The front porch was swept often and I did that sometimes, but I guess there was never any hard work for me to do, the way my parents worked on their farms as children.

Front Porch Stories

Most of my mother's family lived on Cyrus Creek, with one brother on the other side of the hill called Tom's Creek. Her youngest brother lived in Michigan. I had several cousins close to my age and we played together often. In the summertime, days were so hot you could hardly breathe. Houses were not air-conditioned, and neither were cars.

On Saturday evenings we hopped into Daddy's old black Chevy and visited my grandparents. I always called them "Mom and Pop Scarberry." They lived up a graveled road off Cyrus Creek. It has been paved now for many years, but then, the dust boiled up as cars traveled over the bumpy road. Their little white framed house had an L shaped front porch with a swing on one side and wooden chairs on the other. I can still picture Mom Scarberry sitting in the swing, with her short little legs swinging back and forth like a child's. The front porch was the gathering place for my mother, father, aunts, uncles, and grandparents to laugh, talk, tell jokes and stories.

Pop Scarberry was a master storyteller and he would usually get it started with a tale. There were lots of funny stories told, and much laughter. By dark they had turned to ghost stories. The best part is that they were always told as "true." My cousins and I always headed for the front porch to listen. The following are stories that I remember, or that were told to me as I tried to recall some of them.

Pop Scarberry's Ford Model T

(told to me by my uncle, Merle Scarberry)

My grandfather, Lewis Brillie Scarberry (Uncle Merle's father) bought a 1924 Ford Model T automobile. It wasn't new, but It was new to him. It was a two-seater and had a magneto, rather than a battery. He and his oldest son, Virgil, had gone to Hebron Baptist Church that night, driving the car. On the way home, the car lights went out. Since it was pitch dark, Pop couldn't see to drive. He stopped the car and told my Uncle Virgil (who was ten or twelve years old) that he would have to walk to the William Burge place and borrow a kerosene lantern. Since the Burge home was a half-mile away, it was a total of a mile, going to and coming back.

Well, Virgil made it back, carrying the lantern. Pop's idea was that he would drive by the light from the lantern. Virgil was to walk along beside the car, holding it so he could see. All went well for a few minutes until Pop ran over Virgil's leg! This disruption caused the fire to go out in the lantern and Pop could no longer see. Cars were very light in those days, and Virgil was not hurt, so Pop told him he would have to go back to William Burge's house and get him to light the lantern again.

Poor Virgil set out walking. He finally made it back, out of breath, and they were going to try it once more. When Pop cranked up the car again, lo and behold, the lights came back on!

Katie Howard's Curse and the Cat

(about a "real witch" as I remember Pop telling it)

We lived in a farmhouse out in the country. I was about ten years old. Down the road was where an old lady named Katie Howard lived. People stayed away from her because they believed she was a witch. Strange things happened and people thought Katie had something to do with those happenings.

One afternoon, there was a knock on our door. It was early winter, and we had a roaring fire in the fireplace. I went to the door, and there stood Katie Howard. I was scared, but my father came into the room, saw it was Katie, and invited her in. She had never been to our house before and I didn't know why she was there. As she sat on our couch, she spotted the family cat curled up on a rug in front of the fireplace. She pointed a crooked finger at the big cat and said, "Mr. Scarberry, why don't you give me that cat?" My father replied "No—that's our family cat and a good mouser. We want to keep him."

Katie stood up, and in a menacing voice said, "Mr. Scarberry, I WANT that cat!" Again, my father refused, and she said "If you don't give me that cat, you're going to be sorry." He said "Katie Howard, you might scare some people but you don't scare me. I'm keeping the cat."

She turned and walked out, hurrying down the road. She was no sooner out of sight when the big gray cat on the rug woke up, gave a big stretch, then turned and leaped into the open fireplace. Before we could get it out, it burned to death. We always believed Katie put her curse on our cat to get even because she couldn't have it.

Katie Howard: How to Become a Witch

There was a brother and sister who had heard about the witch, Katie Howard. Instead of fearing her, they admired her ability to do witchcraft. They wanted to be like her, so they paid her a visit. The girl asked Katie Howard,

"What can we do to become witches like you?"

"Sure you want to put curses on people the way I can?" Katie asked.

"Oh yes. That's what we want," her brother agreed.

"Well dearies," she said, "this is what you do. Climb to the top of the hill closest to you, and every morning, curse the sun as it rises. Do this for seven mornings in a row. On the seventh morning, go home and look in the mirror."

So the two young people did as they were told. On the seventh morning (Sunday) they were anxious to find out what would happen.

They both ran into their house and to the mirror hanging on the wall. Instead of their own images, they saw Satan himself in the mirror, laughing mockingly at them.

They were so frightened, they ran out screaming. Never again did they try to become witches like Katie Howard.

Katie Howard and the Calf

(told to me by Uncle Merle)

It seems Katie Howard always wanted something that Pop Scarberry's father owned. This time she wanted his calf. He did not want to give it away, and especially not to her. As before, when she did not get her way, she warned him, "You'll be sorry, Mr. Scarberry."

A few days later, the seemingly healthy calf got sick and died. In those days, people wasted nothing they could use to feed their families, so they began the process of dressing the meat.

When they cut open the calf, there, in its stomach, was a very large rock! Not only that, but there was moss covering the rock. They knew for sure that old Katie had put her curse on the calf.

The Haunted Porch

As a young boy, Pop Scarberry's family moved to a house that was haunted, according to people who had lived there before. However, they needed a home, so they moved into the old two-story farmhouse.

The first night, tired from moving, they were all in bed sleeping. Suddenly, a rocking sound started. It woke up Pop's father first (his name was "Noah"). He looked at the clock and saw it was midnight. Then his mother woke up. Noah got up, pulled on a pair of trousers, and went downstairs to find the source of the noise.

When he was downstairs, it was apparent the noise was coming from the front porch. He eased the door open, expecting to see a chair rocking from the sharp wind, but there was no chair. In fact, there was nothing at all on the porch, and the noise had stopped.

Noah Scarberry went back to bed and the rocking started again. Numerous times he made a trip to the porch, only to find the noise stopped when the door opened. Soon as it started, he would raise up in the bed. "Noah," his wife said (she pronounced his name 'No-ee') "where you going?" His reply was always the same: "I'm goin' to kill the Devil."

They finally had to move so they could get some much needed rest from this mischievous ghost that haunted their front porch.,

Omen

(a true story my mother used to tell, in her words)

Everyone was getting ready to go to church that evening. I had a letter to finish writing, so I told Mom, Pop and my brothers to go without me, and I would be there shortly. I was a teenager at the time.

I took the old kerosene lantern and started walking to church. As I neared the Swann house along the way, I could hear a child crying. It sounded so pitiful. The house was totally dark, but the child continued crying as I walked on past the house.

When I got to church, there sat the Swann family and their children. I believe there were six of them. I went over to Mrs. Swann and told her one of her children at her house was crying. She looked down the row of seated children and said, "All my young'uns are here. There's none at home."

One week later the youngest Swann child, a little girl, fell ill suddenly and died. We always thought that what I heard that night was an omen of her coming death.

POP SCARBERRY

Pop's eyes twinkled like
Twin star sapphires
On a dusky summer evening.

A stately giraffe who peered
Down at his grandchildren,
Begging for a story,

About the young boy who
Climbed the old oak tree
To escape being punished

Only to fall asleep dreaming
Of wild bears
And hitting the ground with a
Rude awakening.

He brought tears of laughter
And shrieks of fright
With tall tales and "true" stories
Of witches and ghosts.

B.B.

Childhood Sketches

Before dark, at Pop Scarberry's house, my cousins and I always played games. Sometimes it was *Lemonade, Tag, Black Snake,* or *Ring Around the Rosies.*

One evening as our parents all sat on the front porch laughing and talking, my cousins and I were just across the road on the bridge in front of Becky's house. We were holding hands and dancing in a circle, singing *Ring Around the Rosies.* Suddenly, the elastic in my little cotton panties broke and they fell to the ground. I was wearing a little gathered skirt and halter top, but *all* my relatives on the porch saw me lose my drawers and the laughter was so-oo embarrassing! Grabbing my panties and pulling them up, I held onto them and ran around behind the house. My mother came around the house with a safety pin. She was still laughing!

If we were not playing games, one of the things we cousins liked to do was catch frogs that hatched in a ditch in our grandparents' driveway. At the edge of dark, the peepers would begin their serenade. We learned to creep up so quietly that they could not hear us. Then, a tiny croaker could be grabbed from the water. I did not want to put my hand in the yucky muddy water, so my cousin caught one and placed it in my hand. I was so excited to be holding a frog that I had to show it to Mom Scarberry, who was in the house. I carried it carefully inside with a hand cupped over it for security. As I lifted my hand for Mom to see, the frog suddenly leaped out, hopping across the floor. Mom shrieked and got far away. But then, I was afraid to pick it up and the tiny thing continued terrorizing my grandmother until my cousin, Ronnie, came in and captured it. He took it outside, to Mom Scarberry's great relief.

I Remember

I remember a quiet little girl who could sit for hours in a child-sized chair, drawing pictures. Later, as she learned to read, that same child sat in the same little chair and read slowly at first, then with more confidence as the words began to take on meaning.

There were happy days at play with first cousins, joining hands and skipping in a circle to "ring around the rosies." The last one down had to name her boyfriend. Rolling her eyes and giggling, she always named the same boy (R.T., who happened to be a teenager).

Dusky evenings were a delight to this child, sitting on the porch swing, listening to Grandpa's ghost stories, with the spring peepers serenading the evening, and whippoorwills calling their monotonous song.

When I was about seven, Daddy bought me a beautiful, green, two-tone bicycle with a leather seat. He bought my sister, Phyllis, a new dark blue bike. I was thrilled until I realized I could not ride it—there were no training wheels. It took a long time, but I finally learned how to ride in the yard.

The next morning, following my mastering the bike, my sister Phyllis and our cousin decided to ride to *Jeffrey's Store* on Route 60. "I want to go, too. I can ride now," I begged. My sister did not want me tagging along, but Mother relented, "Let her go with you, but watch out for cars."

All went well until we were on our way home. While going around a curve, I cut the steering too sharply and went sliding over, landing beside the road. I got skinned knees and elbows and a few bruises from that first bike ride.

I had many toys, but nothing close to what children have today. Every Christmas brought a new doll. I kept each one and named it. I had one named Wanda, another named Kathy, a new-born baby, Tiny Tears, Cinderella, Red Riding Hood, a Betsy Wetsy, and many others. I had doll clothes we bought at the ten cent stores. There was a jump rope, jacks, Chinese checkers, dominoes, a red cash register, a doll buggy, a doll high chair, a small baby-grand piano, a two story metal doll house, and several other toys. I loved crayons and coloring books, as well as my Little Golden Books. I had three stuffed animals. One was a monkey I called Zippy.

One thing I especially loved was a red record player, made for children. Because it cost more than many of my toys I had to wait awhile for it. Finally, it was mine! Every time we went shopping, I was allowed to buy a new story record. Eventually, the collection built until there were many, many musical story records. I loved to sit listening and singing with *Pinocchio, The Three Little Pigs,* and *Jonah and the Whale.*

In the fifties, comic books were popular with children. We traded them after reading. I loved *Little Lulu* best. Other characters included: *Tom and Jerry, Tweety and Sylvester, Hot Stuff* (the little devil), and *Archie,* as well as westerns and classics. I think there was some value to comic books because children actually read for entertainment.

Sometime between first and second grade, my father bought me a beautiful little maple roll-top desk and chair. It had compartments and a drawer for my supplies. I convinced Daddy that I needed it to do my homework. *This little desk is still one of my most treasured items from my childhood, and has its place in my home. Both my children played with it and my little granddaughter played with it as well.*

Sidewalk skates were fun and many children had them. They came with a skate key to adjust the length and the width. You wore them with your shoes on. Since Cyrus Creek was a rural area, we had no public sidewalks for skating, so the sidewalks in our yards were about the only place we could use them.

My Big Sisters

Dodie entertained me while Mother was busy. She showed me how to make a ladies hat with a large redbud leaf. We pierced the leaf with a sharp stick and threaded wild flowers through the holes. We placed them on our heads and laughed. We made ropes of clover blossoms and little dolls out of hollyhock blooms.

When we were inside, we listened to the radio. Dodie loved music and sometimes sang along. I can remember Patti Page singing *Tennessee Waltz,* Hank Williams' mournful *Your Cheatin' Heart,* and Patti's *Mockingbird Hill.* Dodie sang that song and I loved it.

Dodie made everything fun time. She read story books to me, made picnic lunches and took me across the creek to a field to eat. When she made boiled eggs, she even ate the yolk from my egg because she knew I didn't like it—just the white. If she went to visit someone, she took me along.

Christmas was especially fun. Dodie was always the one who chopped down our tree. She took me on the hill with her. The pine tree we selected was always bare on one side, but no problem; she put that side against the wall. One time, we spotted sleigh tracks in the snow. Dodie told me it must be Santa's sleigh and he was headed up to our cousins' house (on top of a hill).

As Christmas neared, I was reminded that Santa was watching to see if I was naughty or nice. One cold day, I stepped out on the porch and yelled, "Santa, if you're out there, please bring me some candy to let me know." A short while later Dodie said, "Do you think Santa left you any candy?" I ran to the front door, looked out, and on the front porch banister stood three little wax Santa's, filled with sweet red syrup. After this, I was sure Santa Claus was watching and listening. Sometimes he would leave me a red sucker, the kind with a loop handle stick, or little striped peanut butter logs.

One day I heard a *thump-thump* on a window beside the fireplace. I looked up and there was a new-born baby doll at the window—the kind I wanted for Christmas. I ran out the front door and around the house, but did not see Santa Claus or the doll. That doll was under the tree on Christmas!

My doll needed a bassinet, so Dodie made one. She took a peck basket and covered it with leftover wallpaper. She used a scalloped border around the top of the basket, which looked quite fancy. She used a wire hanger to fashion some legs so it would stand a little higher. Another time, she made a doll table with a maraschino cherry jar and a candy box. The jar was the pedestal for the table.

My half-sisters usually took me along wherever they went. I recall walking a long way to their aunt's house. I believe she was their father's sister. She was an older lady and wore an apron, as women did back then. She had a pawpaw tree in her yard and she told us we could have all the pawpaws we wanted. We gathered them up and put them in a brown crock jar so we could carry them home. She said we could have the jar.

A scary time I remember is when Dova and Phyllis took me with them one evening up the hollow where our grandparents lived. On the way home, it was getting dark and they were trying to hurry before it was totally dark. Suddenly, we heard a loud scream up on the hill, in the woods. They stopped and stared at each other and Dova said, "It's a wildcat, let's run!" Each of them grabbed my hand and away we flew. I don't believe my poor little feet even touched the ground until we got home!

Phyllis took me with her to visit a friend down the road. I must have been three or four—not old enough to walk on the road alone. Well, I got tired and wanted to go home, but my sister kept talking and ignored me. So, I took off walking home all by myself. She did not even know it. Mother was shocked to see me come home alone and told me I could have been hit by a car. I told her that when a car came by, "I got way, way 'ober' in the grass."

One day I begged for a new outfit for my doll, Wanda. My sister, Phyllis, told me if I would just be quiet, she would sew a dress for her. She was in the outbuilding for the better part of the day, using Mother's old Singer treadle sewing machine. When she came out, Wanda was wearing a yellow sleeveless dotted Swiss dress, a matching wide brim hat, and a little drawstring purse was hanging on her arm. Phyllis had used red rick-rack for trim. It was so pretty and I couldn't wait to show off Wanda.

My middle sister, Emalene, was the sister I did not really know until years later. She married young and had four children and they kept her quite busy.

Little Sister

My mother fostered several children when I was young, one at a time. One child she kept was a little baby boy named David. Mother never had a son of her own and she grew to love him dearly. She cried for days after the social worker took him to place in another home or with his parent(s).

I believe the oldest child she kept was four years old. When I was nearly eight years old, the social worker brought Mother a new-born baby girl, born just the night before. Rosa got to stay with us for several years, which was unusual. Mother and Daddy loved her very much and were finally allowed to adopt her when she was seven. Mother bought her a cute little dress to wear to court for the adoption. Rosa said it was her *graduation dress.*

Rosa told me her earliest memory was on a Christmas Eve. When we went somewhere at this time, Santa would come while we were away. We were hoping he would come if we went to Dodie's house. "I was about three," she said. "You were small for your age and I was tall, so I was nearly as big as my big sister. We put on our winter coats and you took me on your back (piggyback) to Dova's house. There was no snow accumulation, but big snowflakes were falling all around, just right for Christmas."

The Rooster

My earliest playmates (not related to me) were two girls who moved into a house nearby. One was close to my age and the other was two years older. We had fun and played well together except for one time.

At Easter time in the fifties, you could buy live, colored chicks. They were so cute and fuzzy, and they were sprayed with colors of blue, pink, green or purple. I always begged for two Easter *biddies* and usually got them, as Mother had a small hen house with a few laying hens. These biddies grew very fast and they were always roosters, not hens. My cute green chick grew into a mean old thing that loved to flog me. I was terrified of him, so I began carrying a stick to defend myself every time I went outside. When he came at me with his neck outstretched, wanting blood, I swatted at him with my stick and he retreated.

One day, carrying my stick, I walked the path to my friend Vera's house to play. She was in the backyard, tossing rocks into the deep hole of water in the creek. Vera saw my stick and said,

"Let me see that stick." I gave it to her and she threw it into the deep water hole. There it floated, irretrievable.

"Why'd you have to go and do that?" I asked. She laughed and replied,

"I wanted to." I remember getting angry and saying,

"Now I don't have anything to fight off the rooster!"

Vera laughed and I hit her! She hit me back. I hit her again. I don't know how long this would have gone on if her mother had not seen us through the window and yelled at us. We had not yet started school, so we were under six years in age.

I ran home, scared by what I had done, never even giving a thought to that old rooster lurking around. Mother asked, "Why did you come home so early?" I said, "I just didn't feel like playing." She learned the truth from our neighbor. Mother did not punish me for fighting. She knew how scared I was of that rooster, and why I carried the stick. She did, however, make me very ashamed of hitting my friend.

Cats

The most wonderful thing I had in my childhood was a kitten. Pop Scarberry gave me a black long-haired kitten. Their black cat had a litter every spring. Mother told me to keep Smokey in the outbuilding (where she did the laundry). This building held the wringer washer, an old kitchen stove for canning with the pressure cooker, an old Singer treadle sewing machine, and shelves of jelly, jams, and apple butter.

When I went in later to get little Smokey, he wasn't there. I called and called and then searched everywhere. I started crying and Mother came and helped me look. She was afraid he had gotten into the open drain where she put the hose to empty the washing machine. After much searching and crying (on my part), Mother said, "Well look-ee here," as she held up a little black fluff with blue eyes. He was hiding behind a jar of apple butter.

After Smokey, there was another black kitten named Midnight. Then there was Frisky, a white spotted kitten that Phyllis and I found on the road one day. Frisky had only one litter of kittens in her long life-time. People never spayed or neutered their pets back then, and I am not sure it was even done. We were lucky she didn't have more. I kept a little yellow kitten from Frisky's litter and named her Susie. However, by the time I learned Susie was a tomcat, he already knew his name. He was a boy named *Susie!* My kitties were tolerant, for the most part. When I dressed them in doll dresses and bonnets and took them for rides in my doll buggy, they went along with it.

Cats were and still are my favorite little friends. I have included three stories about "cats" in my adult life after the conclusion of FRONT PORCH SKETCHES.

Playing in the Creek

Every kid should have a creek to play in. I spent many hours every summer in the creek catching crawdads in a can, coloring rocks, and digging blue clay mud from the bank to make little bowls and vases. One summer, I sculpted a very realistic bust of "Caesar." It took several days of stacking and molding before I was satisfied with it. I let it dry for weeks, and then I sprayed it with an old can of gold paint I found in the garage.

The creek bank was a great place to make a playhouse. We used old boards to make the border of the house, and we used "found things" from the trash barrel to put in it. We made little mud pies in jar lids and set them out to bake in the sun. We picked pokeberries and smashed them up and put them in little jars we found. It looked just like real jam! Usually, before I tired of my playhouse in the creek, a summer storm would cause the creek to fill and swell with muddy-colored water and it gushed through, taking my playhouse away. Many things washed down the creek when it was up. I once saw a box turtle floating swiftly on the waves with its head out, looking as though it were enjoying the ride. Sometimes a big log or tree got caught crossways and caused a buildup that couldn't wash through. My father would get the rake or hoe and punch and pull until he broke through the jam and the water could flow again.

In the winter the creek froze over and provided a good surface for skating. None of us had ice skates, but we would run and slide on the ice in our rubber boots. The more we slid, the slicker it became, until it was hard to stand up without falling.

Dodie Came Back

Did I tell about how pretty my big sister Dodie was? Her hair was a gold shade of blonde. She wore deep red lipstick and red nail polish. Sometimes she would paint my small fingernails with the same red as hers. In spite of the makeup, Dodie was a bit tomboyish and liked to hike in the woods and sometimes even climb a tree. She also had a quick temper. I was once told that she threw a clod of dirt and hit a chicken in the head. It fell over dead. It was Mother's chicken and Dodie was mad that it got out of the coop. However, she never once used her temper on me.

When I was six years old, on my birthday, my beloved Dodie got married and moved away. I couldn't believe she would leave me. I missed her terribly. She promised to let me come and stay a few days with her in the little rented house on Darnell Road off West Pea Ridge. I did get to stay before school started. While I was there one day, Dodie asked,

"Do you want to try this new strawberry soda pop?"

"Sure," I replied. She handed me a small glass of red liquid and I quickly drank it all. It was delicious—much better than the Sun Crest orange I liked! I gave a big burp and asked for more.

"We don't have any more. You want to walk down to the store with me and get some?"

"Yes—can we go now?"

"Okay, but you have to hold my hand so a car won't hit you."

"I promise, Dodie."

While at the store, Dodie also bought me a red lollipop. We called them *suckers,* then. She purchased two bottles of Sun Crest strawberry pop. We walked back to her house, a bit tired after that long walk. Then we drank our strawberry soda to quench our dry throats. It helped ease my loneliness by getting to stay with Dodie for a while.

I had to get my dreaded school shots before starting school. There were no preschools or kindergartens back then—you started in first grade. My father promised that if I didn't cry when I got the shots, he would buy me a little blue pedal car that we had seen in the window of Brady's Hardware Store in Barboursville. Now this was a bribe, I know, but I'm sure my daddy was remembering how I screamed when Dr. Bourn gave me a shot once before, when I had measles that would not break out.

Well, as Daddy was fond of telling people, "Brenda sat up like a little soldier and got her shots without shedding a tear." I loved that little blue pedal car and played with it until my legs finally grew too long to fit under the steering wheel.

Dodie moved back to Cyrus Creek and lived beside us (with a lot in-between). Her husband, who was building a trade as a bricklayer, built them a small house. She had a new baby boy she named Darrell. She still had time for me, though. She had a TV before my parents ever bought one, and she let me watch it anytime. I watched *Kukla, Fran, and Ollie,* and *Ding Dong School* with Miss Frances. One day Miss Frances asked on her show:

"Do you have a wagon?"

"Yes," I replied.

"You do? What color is it—is it *red?"*

"No, it's green," I answered.

"Oh—is it *green*?"

From then on, I just *knew* people on TV could hear me, so I often talked back to them.

Sometimes when my cousin, Kathy, would come to play with me, we often ended up going to Dodie's house. She was always playing games with us like *I Spy,* or *Button, Button, Who's Got the Button?* Sometimes it was a card game of *Old Maid.* There was a TV show in the morning called *Bride and Groom.* Dodie would decide which of us would be the bride the following day. It was a pretend game that we loved. One day when I was to be the bride, the girl was a beautiful blonde in a lovely gown and her groom was quite handsome. I was happy that I was the *bride* that day.

By the time I was in third grade, we finally had a TV. It was brand new, in a boxy mahogany cabinet, and it had a set of what we called *rabbit ears* on top. These were to get reception on the three channels. Often, they had to be adjusted when channels were changed. We always had good shows to watch on TV. There were only three channels to watch. Some of the programs we enjoyed were:

The Red Skelton Hour
Milton Beryl Show
Dinah Shore (Chevy Show)
Dragnet

Situation comedies were everyone's favorites. They included:

My Little Margie
Father Knows Best
Make Room for Daddy
I Love Lucy
Leave it to Beaver

Then there were the westerns. Now there is almost never a western to watch. Some of the good ones were:

Tales of Wells Fargo
Death Valley Days
Have Gun, Will Travel
Bat Masterson
Restless Gun
Wagon Train

Maybe it's nostalgia, but television was so much better than it is now. Whether we watched TV or did something else, it was always fun at Dodie's house.

Me, 1 year old

Big sister, Dodie and me

Me, with Dodie

Older me with Dova

Lewis Brillie and Helen Scarberry, Grandparents

Sunday School Class, me, front row left

Mother, dressed for church

Sisters, Phyllis, Dova and me

Daddy, Mother and me

Pedal cars! Me and Darrell

Me and baby Rosa

Mr. Stallo, teacher and principal

Me, 6th grade

Me, little David, and Daddy

5th and 6th Grade Class, Watson Elementary, 1956-57,
Me, front row L-R #4

Old Watson School 1867 - 1963

Cyrus Creek Church, Easter Sunday, 1955

Teka

"Lady" Clarissa

Marissa and Susie

Marissa, crossing her legs

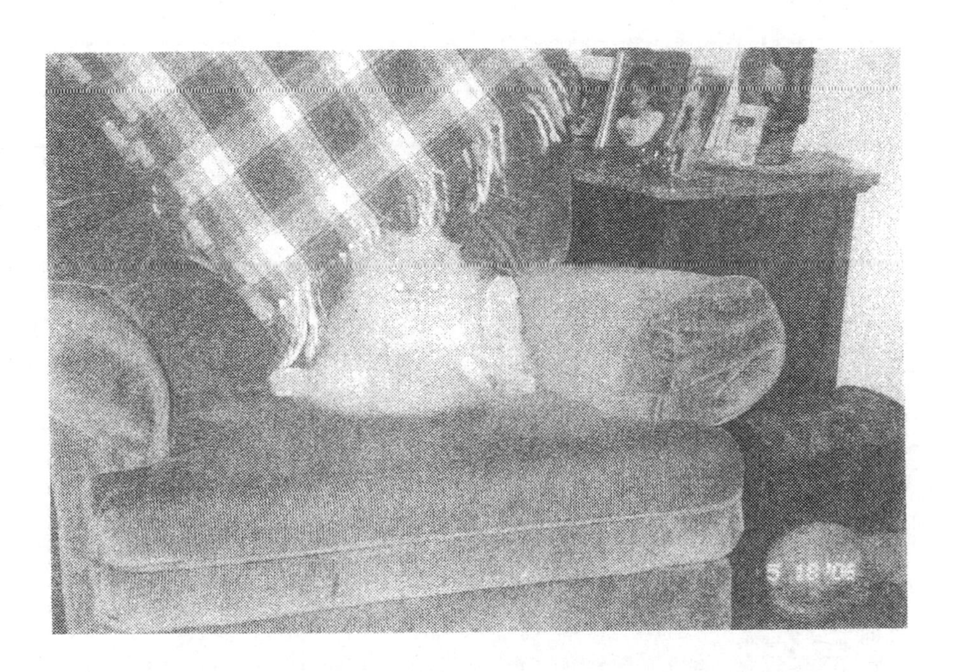

Susie, favorite way of sitting

Grade School Sketches

Watson School 1951

Watson Elementary was a four-room frame school. It served grades one through six. The room that served as first and second grade was divided from the cafeteria by moveable coat closets. There was a separate third and fourth grade room, and fifth and sixth grades were in one room. The main hallway had a water fountain and a large sink, where we washed our hands. Toilets were outside—one for boys and one for girls. The school floors were oiled wood that always had a certain school smell. In fourth, fifth and sixth grades, the desks and chairs were bolted to the floor. These are the ones now sold as antiques. The other grades all had tables with cubby holes underneath and separate wooden chairs.

Mrs. Tackett, First Grade

School was scary at first, but my cousin was in second grade in the same room with me. Mrs. Tackett was a good teacher and I learned to read from a green textbook. The two children in this book were *Jim and Judy* and they had a dog and a cat by the names of *Tags and Twinkle.* I loved when Mrs. Tackett lined us up in front of the supply cabinet and gave each of us a hand-sized ball of oil modeling clay. It was always green or gray—no other colors. It smelled good and I loved to roll it out and make things with it.

It was in first grade that I received my first kiss. My friend, Linda, and I were out on the playground walking around. A little boy in my room called "Hoppy" came running in the opposite direction. He stopped, kissed me on the forehead, and ran away. All I remember about Hoppy was that he dressed in a black cowboy suit and played *cowboy* on the playground. The nickname "Hoppy" was after the (then) famous cowboy, Hopalong Cassidy. Every time Linda saw Hoppy, she would say in a sing-song voice, *"Hoppy loves Brenda, Hoppy loves Brenda."*

I was by far the smallest girl in my first grade class. At recess, a big sixth grade boy with the first name of Carl started calling me *grasshopper.* Every day, if he saw me on the playground, it was "Hi Grasshopper." I told my big sister Dodie that I did not like for this big boy to call me this name and I wanted him to stop. She told me, "Well, the next time he calls you Grasshopper, just say: Hi there, Tobacco Worm" (that was the ugliest critter she could think of). I think I tried it once, but eventually he stopped calling me "grasshopper" on his own.

Mrs. Tackett was a very wise teacher. One day, I shyly went to her and told her about something that had disappeared from my desk. The "something" happened to be a very small inflated Easter rabbit with his legs together which formed an O. Sticking inside this O was a package of *Clove* chewing gum. Daddy had bought it for me the day before, at the little grocery store he frequented.

After lunch, we were all seated at our tables and Mrs. Tackett began talking. She said that someone had stolen from another child's desk. She had a short stack of index cards, and one would be given to each child. We were to turn them over, and it should be blank, unless there was a red "X" on it. This X would define the guilty person who had wrongfully taken something that was not their own.

I had quickly figured out that Mrs. Tackett had no intention of naming me as the one who was stolen from and she gave me a card as well. The little girl who sat directly across from me turned over her card and there was a big red X on it. She looked scared. I remember her name, but will refer to her as "CW." She asked the girl beside her to trade cards and then the next on the other side. Nobody wanted the red X. Well, I cannot remember what was said to CW, but she learned very quickly that she would be found out if she stole from someone.

Mrs. Tackett then returned my rabbit with the package of gum, which had been opened. One stick was missing, but I got it back.

Mrs. Mularky, Mrs. Grizzell, Second Grade

Second grade was awful. I had a young teacher who was pregnant, and she was really short on patience. One thing I would like to forget, but never have, is sitting in a reading circle with Mrs. Mularky. When it was my turn to read, I didn't know the first word that started the sentence, so I said nothing. She told me to begin, but I just sat there, shy and embarrassed because I didn't know the word. She suddenly leaned over, grabbed me by the shoulders and shook me hard while yelling, "Speak to me, speak to me!" Badly frightened, I managed to whisper, "I don't know that word." Thankfully, Mrs. Mularky went on maternity leave and was replaced by Mrs. Grizzell. She was nice and I lost my fear, but I was always bashful around teachers.

Mrs. Ramey, Third Grade

Mrs. Ramey was my third grade teacher. She was a heavy-set woman and very nice. She slipped on an orange peel on the floor one day and fell hard. The students all laughed, but I didn't. I knew she must have hurt a lot.

For music in third grade, we listened to Miss Martin on the radio. She was a fill-in for music because we had no regular music teacher as elementary schools have now. Because Miss Martin sang opera, we children did not care about listening. I think Mrs. Ramey knew this, so she had us do a musical in class. We practiced every day as we listened and sang along with *The Raggle Taggle Town Singers.* Each table was assigned to sing as: the old yellow dog, the fat cat, the donkey, and the red rooster. Every day after lunch, we practiced. My table was the rooster.

Cock-a-doodle-doo, cock-a-doodle-doo, my master's going to make me into stew, me into stew, me into stew, My master's going to make me into stew, he says I'm too old to crow—in the morning, he says I'm too old to crow. I think we all enjoyed this musical and it sure beat listening to Miss Martin.

In the afternoon while waiting for the bus, several children from other rooms would gather in Mrs. Ramey's room. Eddie, a boy in my room with a cute chubby face, was sitting at a table when a fourth grade boy came over carrying a thick, hard-backed book. He stood behind Eddie and said,·"Watch this." He then brought the book down hard on Eddie's head. Eddie just sat there smiling to show it didn't hurt. The older boy repeated this a second time and was getting ready to come down on Eddie's head again when I said, "Stop—you're going to hurt him!" Others heard me, so they all teased me about Eddie being my boyfriend. I guess Eddie believed it too, because he was always really sweet to me. On Valentine's Day, Eddie's valentine was the largest and nicest one I received. The following school year, Eddie did not come back to Watson—his family moved. *As I recall this, I wonder whether or not his brain suffered trauma from those hard licks on his head.*

During the year, someone abandoned a little gray tiger-striped kitten in the school yard. Mrs. Ramey brought it in for us to pet, and asked who would like to have the kitten. Every hand went up, including mine. She decided I should have it and I felt so privileged! My father picked me up from school on his way home from work. I got in the car with my precious little bundle of fur wrapped in my new red sweater. I couldn't wait to show it to my mother. When we got home, that sweet little kitten had pooped a mess in my brand new sweater and Mother nearly had a fit! She *did* let me keep the kitty, though.

Mrs. Ramey rented a little house on Cyrus Creek and walked to school while she taught at Watson for several years.

Miss Harrison, Fourth Grade

Miss Harrison was an unmarried lady and about the oldest teacher I ever knew. She brought a thermos of warm milk for her lunch every day. We understood she had stomach ulcers and this was all her stomach would tolerate. I loved Miss Harrison. She was small and thin and wore *old lady* dresses. Two of the mean boys in my class gave her such a hard time. They would wait until she was standing at the blackboard teaching, and then make weird noises. Her nose would turn red and she would pick up her ruler and walk back to the offending boys. “Hold out your hand,” she would demand. Each boy would hold out his hand, palm up; as she brought the ruler down, they would jerk away their hands at the last second, grinning from ear to ear. Both boys were equally horrible. Miss Harrison’s nose would get redder and redder. No wonder she had ulcers!

That fourth grade year, I learned my multiplication table and how to do division. I also learned the Twenty-Third Psalm, which Miss Harrison had us recite every morning. I have never forgotten it. She also noticed my ability to draw and how much I enjoyed art. At a parent/teacher conference she told my mother: “Send that little girl to college. She’ll make a fine art teacher someday.” I believe that little teacher could foretell the future!

Mr. Stallo, Fifth and Sixth Grade

When I started to school, Mr. Virgil Collins was the principal. Then there was Mr. Don Davidson, then Mr. Bill Stallo. In the rural schools, the principal also was a teacher. So Mr. Stallo was my fifth and sixth grade teacher. Everyone loved Mr. Stallo and he loved all the kids. He was thirty-two at the time and the father of two little boys. His wife taught in another school.

Every morning, Mr. Stallo wrote the day’s agenda on the blackboard. We didn’t do every subject every day, but by the end of the week, we had done it all. Mr. Stallo would sometime slip in "talent show" on the agenda. It was always in the afternoon, so we had time to decide what talent to perform over lunch hour. Mostly, girls would sing a solo or a duet. One boy, Bobby, was always a stand-up comic and he was good at it. *Singing the Blues* was popular at the time. I was so shy, I don't know where I got the courage, but I sang that song in the talent show. Mr. Stallo just made everything so much fun!

For a writing lesson, Mr. Stallo would assign us a page to write from our reader. If there was a picture on that page, we had to draw and color it as well. That became our art lesson. I loved both, and kept several colors of bottled ink in my desk: red, green, blue, and black. I had a red ink pen that I dipped into the bottle to fill the nib. My handwriting was good and I knew it, so the ink was my way of showing off a little. Today, many schools no longer teach handwriting. Everything is printed by hand or done on computers. Handwriting is fast becoming a lost art.

I remember one day when Mr. Stallo called a boy up to his desk and handed back his writing paper assignment. He asked him to read it to him. The boy stuttered and stammered and only read a word or two. Mr. Stallo could not keep the grin off his face. The boy said, "I can't read it." Mr. Stallo replied, "Now Lester, if *you* can't read it, how in the world do you think *I* can?"

When the weather was nice, Mr. Stallo would sometimes go to Orchard Hills Golf in Barboursville to practice during lunch hour. He would select one student each time and that student could then choose three others to go. We would pile into his old faded green car and leave the school, thinking we were special. Teachers would be in deep trouble if they did this in today's schools.

We often went on field trips, always within walking distance of the school. Once we went to Coovert's farm to see the newborn animals. We went to Erwin's mink farm, and once to what is now Indian Meadows. The houses had not been built yet, but due to excavating, there was a large stone quarry. We looked for and gathered rocks. Mr. Stallo carried a cloth bag of rocks back to the school room, took a hammer and broke them up. There were the usual rocks like quartz and granite, sandstone, conglomerate, shale and others, but one quartz rock had real gold deposits in it. He explained that because the rock was so hard, it would be difficult to extract the gold, so it would not be worth much. He gave each of us a piece of every rock and we glued them inside a box and labeled them, to make a collection. This field of study made a big impression on me. I have since always had an interest in rocks.

One day Mr. Stallo brought a can of white paint to school. After school, he taped off the blacktop to make hopscotches. He worked for several days until all were completed. We had about six of them. They were in use daily and enjoyed by all grades.

Mr. Stallo also taught us how to march—military style. Looking back now, he most surely was in the military service. He taught us to keep in step with *left, left, left-right, left.* We did cadence count *1—2—3—4—1-2—3-4! You had a good home and you left—your right. You had a good home and you left—your right—sound off 1-2 sound off 1-2 cadence count —1-2-3-4, 1-2, 3-4!* Mr. Stallo kept us marching until we were all familiar with every command, and we had a good workout.

In the winter, schools never closed for snow. The school bus garages just put chains on the bus wheels and they ran. Many times I remember the bus sliding on past me as I waited beside the road to get on. It was that slippery!

We had fun outside at school, sliding down the bank behind the building on cardboard that bread was delivered in. We built snowmen and snow forts. Mr. Stallo was always right out there with us, having as much fun as the kids.

Although Mr. Stallo was nice, he did not let kids get away with anything. One day, he caught J and N out behind the boy's toilet. They were smoking cigarettes! Their punishment was five licks with the paddle to each other with Mr. Stallo's *board of education.* He warned them that if the licks were not hard enough, he would take over the paddle and do it for them. The rest of us watched from our desks as first one, then the other, bent over and had his rear end paddled. Mr. Stallo warned twice—"harder." They obeyed, for they knew it would be much worse from the teacher.

I was a picky eater and Mr. Stallo noticed. On a day when we had pinto beans and cornbread for lunch, I didn't even touch the food on my tray. He said, "Brenda, you can't go outside until you eat your beans." Well, I never did eat that awful stuff at home—so how could I eat it at school? I sat there and sat and sat and finally the bell rang. Recess was over and I had missed it all! Mr. Stallo stood and said, "You can go empty your tray now." He had a resigned smile on his face, as if to say, *it was worth a try.*

There was a polio epidemic in the fifties and people feared for their children. They gave the polio vaccine in school. You had to have written permission from a parent to receive it. Mother had read in *Life Magazine* that the serum was made from some part of monkeys. This did not seem right to her and when they gave the polio vaccine at Watson, Mother refused to let me have it. Fortunately, polio passed me by.

Daddy bought me a little *Brownie* camera when I was in fifth grade. I was so proud of it. Several of the pictures in this book were taken with my Brownie, including the picture of Mr. Stallo.

All through my school days, the paddle was still used for discipline. Mother always said to me as I left for school, "Be good and mind your teacher." I always did, and never once felt the sting of the paddle all through my school years. None of the girls in my class were paddled, as far as I know.

Sometimes on beautiful spring days, my friend, Linda, and I decided to walk home, instead of riding the school bus. It was a mile from Watson Elementary to our homes. In the warm sun, we dawdled, picking wild flowers by the side of the road on the way. We always had nice bouquets for our mothers by the time we got home.

We were halfway home on one particular day when a car stopped and Mr. Hershel Thomas, a man who was a member of our Cyrus Creek church said,

"You girls want a ride?" Linda was tired—we both were, as it was a rather hot day for spring.

"Let's ride, Brenda," she said.

"No—Mother told me to never get in a car with a stranger." So we walked the rest of the way.

Apparently, Mr. Thomas told Mother what I said about not riding with a stranger. He had been a family friend all my life, but Mother forgot to explain what *stranger* meant. They had a big laugh over my cautious nature.

One morning before school, I was bragging about the talents of Aunt Christine. My mother was fifteen when her only sister was born, so she was still young while my mother was "old." My aunt kept her beautiful home spotless. My mother worked all day, but our house was never spotless. My aunt was the best cook, ever. Her coconut cake was out of this world delicious. Mother's coconut cake was so dry you would choke if you did not eat fruit salad with it. My aunt made the best lemonade and egg salad sandwiches when I played with my cousin at her house. She also made awesome pickles in brine in a big crock—they crunched when you ate them—just delicious! I begged Mother to make some like that. She tried several times, but her pickles were always soggy.

Mother must have been hurt about my singing the praises of her sister because she asked "Would you rather have Christine for a mother?" Without hesitating, "Yes" slipped off my tongue.

I went to school, but could not concentrate all day. I knew I had hurt my mother's feelings. When the school day finally ended and I went home, the first thing I did was tell Mother I was sorry.

Just a few years ago at a birthday party for my uncle, my cousin Becky told me her mother was always asking *her* why she couldn't be more like Brenda and keep her clothes neat and clean. I don't remember it, but Becky said she played hard at school and got her clothes so dirty and sometimes ripped. That struck me as quite funny—maybe Mother and Aunt Christine should have traded daughters!

To set things right, Mother did have some talents as a cook. Her apple cobbler was delicious, as were her chicken and dumplings and her Mississippi mud cake. She worked as a school cook for a while at Watson Elementary before I was born.

She was a good mother to me. On the last day of school at Watson Elementary, there was an annual picnic. The parents came and brought the food. Mother always made cheese spread and ham salad sandwiches. She used a grinder, which had to be clamped to a table. In the open top, she fed the cheese, pickles, and pimento, while turning the handle. It came out in delicious strings as it fell into a large bowl. When both bowls were full, she added mayonnaise and mixed, then made dozens of sandwiches. She always made a cake or pie as well.

The hardest thing my mother did for the picnic was carry her large box of picnic goodies for a mile to Watson School. We had one car (like everyone else at that time) and she did not drive anyway, so walking was the only way. She and our neighbor walked together, carrying their heavy boxes to the school, stopping to rest occasionally.

Another thing that comes to mind is Mother making a little majorette costume for me to wear in a second grade performance. The teacher sent instructions home for each parent to make a skirt and cape and a hat from an oatmeal box. It was covered with crepe paper and a string or ribbon was attached to tie under the chin. She also had to buy me a small rubber-tipped baton. She sewed and glued and I was so proud of my little majorette costume. We were lined up in a row across the cafeteria and we marched to John Phillip Sousa music. We learned to listen when there was a slight change in the music. For this, we began *twirling* our batons. None of us knew how to twirl, but it must have been cute to see us trying.

When I was sick, or not feeling well from a cold, my mother gave me a bowl of tomato soup and saltine crackers. It was home-canned tomato juice. She added milk and a pat of butter to it. Even now, when not feeling well, I have tomato soup. I find it comforting.

My mother made cornbread stuffed tomatoes in the summertime. She said only the Scarberry family made them like this. Here is the recipe:

Cornbread Stuffed Tomatoes

Large red tomatoes

Cornbread

Onion

Bell pepper

Slice the top off washed ripe tomatoes. Use grapefruit spoon to hollow out insides, putting in a large bowl. Dice onion and bell pepper into a bowl. Crumble squares of cornbread into bowl and mash together with other ingredients. Salt and pepper to taste. Scoop into tomato shells until heaping full.

Summer Vacation

Every summer, one of the things we always looked forward to was the Bookmobile. Since I lived closer to the church than anyone else, all the kids met at my house and we waited on the front porch. It was so exciting when the Bookmobile finally pulled into the church parking lot. Mr. Powell always drove in all the years I borrowed books in the summer. I could hardly wait for the door to open and that step up into the world of books. It always had a certain smell—the smell of books, I think.

While waiting for the Bookmobile, we discussed whether or not we would join the Summer Reading Club. We always joined.

I had borrowed books from the time I started school. I loved the pictures in the early reader books, but something changed the summer I had finished third grade and would be ready to enter fourth grade in the fall. I had to read books with no pictures. What a bummer! However, I soon discovered these were great books. Instead of pictures to look at while I read, the pictures began forming in my mind. I found this was better than ever! We all read many books and received our certificates with our name and the number of books read.

We had no public swimming pools during my elementary and junior high years—at least not near my house. By the time I reached my early teens, we had the Ona pool, which was not far from home.

Everyone went to swim at the *railroad bridge* or the *falls.* This was the Mud River that flowed at both sites out Blue Sulphur road. There was sand to play in along the sides of the river. If you went to the railroad bridge swimming hole, you had to walk through a cornfield. Then you had to go through weeds down a slippery bank to reach the water. Sometimes you picked up *chiggers* along the way. These were little critters that burrowed into your skin and itched like crazy. I was not allowed to go to the falls often, as it was supposed to have a whirlpool that pulled people down and drowned them. I do not know of anyone who ever got into the whirlpool, but I believe several people drowned at the falls over the years. Mother was always deathly afraid of water and warned me never to go in over my knees. Of course I did—I was a kid! My cousins and I had old inner tubes we used for floats, and we could paddle anywhere we wanted in those.

I went to Dreamland Pool more than once when my cousin, Linda, who was old enough to drive, was allowed to drive the family car. We cousins pitched in fifty cents to help pay for the gasoline. We always had fun!

In the summer, I rode with my cousins or neighbor friends on the road. The traffic was very light in those days, so we could ride a long time without meeting a car. We sometimes rode up Ramsey Hill, or perhaps I should say, we pushed our bikes up Ramsey Hill; it was too steep to ride, and we only had one speed bikes. From there, we would ride on Tom's Creek, and turn left to go to *Brown's Store*. There, we quenched our thirst with grape Nehi or ate a cool ice cream bar or popsicle. We all had to have permission from our mothers to ride that far. We were pretty tired by the time we made it back home.

There was a little store not far down the road from where I lived. It was called *Marcum's Market.* My cousins and I checked out the candy there often. We always had a few coins to spend on Bazooka bubble gum or a nickel for a candy bar. Reese's peanut butter cups were my favorite. They were so much larger for a nickel than they are now at eighty-nine cents. One day, I thought I had twenty-five cents, so I decided to pig-out on a self-treat of five Reese's cups. It turned out my coins came to only twenty-three cents. Mr. Marcum told me to take the candy and bring him the two cents next time. I paid him what I owed the next day. My dad showed me by example to always pay my debts.

My next-door playmates had only one bicycle they shared. I would ride with one of them up and down the road for a long time. Then, as we neared their house, the other one would be waiting beside the road. She would yell, "It's my turn to ride with Brenda now." I would ride again for a long, long, time. Then they would switch places again. I got twice the exercise they did!

One day, Linda and I pulled over, parked our bikes, and sat on the church steps to rest and talk. Suddenly, we heard something inside the church. "What was that?" Linda's eyes grew wide as she heard it too—footsteps coming from inside the church! There were no cars parked in the lot and nobody should have been there at that time! "Maybe it's Jesus," I said. "It could be the Devil—let's get out of here," Linda whispered. We jumped on our bikes and took off. We never knew who or what was inside the church!

So many evenings in the heat of summer, I sat on the front porch with my parents. They always sat in the rocking chairs while I sat on the glider. From the hills, a whippoorwill would begin its static call. Where have they all gone? I seldom hear one now.

Daddy was always the first to turn in. Mother, being very hot natured, never did too well in warm weather. She stayed on the porch and rocked and fanned herself with one of her funeral home fans that were given free to advertise their services. There is one I remember so well; two little children, a boy and a girl, are playing together on the edge of a cliff. Behind them is a beautiful, glowing angel with her arms outstretched, guarding them. *I would love to have one of those fans for a keepsake, but I have never found one.*

One night, I had gone to bed, but could not sleep because it was so hot and I felt sticky. My windows were up with the screens in place, but no air was stirring. Then I heard Mother quietly open the front door and step outside. I knew she was going out to sit awhile and cool off. For some silly reason, I thought it would be fun to jump out and scare her.

I patiently waited and waited, out of sight, beside the front door. After a long time, I heard the chair squeak as my mother rose to come back inside. When she opened the door, I jumped out at her with a loud *boo!* Before I knew what had happened, she shoved me against the wall and I literally saw stars! When she finally realized it was me in the dark, she told me "Don't you *ever* do that again." Believe me, I never did!

Summer Rain

I was never afraid of thunderstorms. These storms usually followed a period of intense summer heat, so rain was always welcome. If there was no lightning, I was allowed to strip down to my panties and run and play in the rain. If one of my cousins happened to be with me, it was even more fun. I also loved sitting on the front porch with my kitty on my lap during rain showers. Kitty was usually tucked inside a doll blanket. He loved it too—I could tell by his little contented purrs.

Something in the rain boosts the mood lifting brain chemical, serotonin. I have always felt exhilarated when it rains. I love taking walks in the rain with my umbrella. Dodie once told me she always looked out the window for me if it was raining. I walked and sang rain songs. Dodie bought me two colorful rain coats in my adult years for my walks in the rain.

RAIN

Rain. Saturating the earth
Overflowing like the welling of tears
Incessant. Pelting green carpets
Relentless in pounding pursuits.
Washing away memories of seasons parched
When the sun had its rein
Cooking dry earth to overdone brownies
Sapping moisture through tentacle straws.
Rain. Black clouds on the horizon
Darken a cerulean sky. Thunder rumbles
A threat as lightning splits
The sky with brilliant light.
Rain. Slashing trees and parting corn
Transforming streams and creeks into
Menacing torrents, snaking over banks
Leaving debris and clutter in the backwater.
Cracked earth, through parched crevices

Speaking its distrust of the sun
Who showed no mercy as the drought
Exercised its dusty authority.
B.B.

When the cicadas began their never-ending song and the lush green of summer faded, it was time to get ready for back-to-school again. I could hardly wait! When we are children, time seems to pass so slowly, especially the summer months. Getting ready meant an exciting trip to Huntington to buy new school clothes.

In the *Huntington Dry Goods* store, racks brimmed with school dresses. There were mostly plaids, and the colors were dark. I never liked dark colors much. They were so dreary. After finding several dresses to try on, I would finally decide which three I liked best. Sometimes instead of three dresses, I would get two dresses and a skirt and blouse. At the shoe store, I tried on shoes until I found a pair just right. I usually got several new pairs of socks and some new underwear, too.

Mother took me to buy new school supplies at *McCroy's* or *Silver's* five and ten cent store. Silver's eventually became *H.L. Green.* We bought a notebook binder, paper, pencils, erasers, and a big box of Crayola crayons—that was best of all! One year, instead of a notebook binder, I begged for a *Lady and the Tramp* book satchel, and got it. There were no backpacks in the fifties.

COLORS

Colors bright, brilliant, intoxicating
Dotting hills and yards

Chill of frosty air,
Blowing and cooling

Crisp, crunchy leaves, twirling
On wild roller coaster rides,

Covering lawns and hills, piling,
Scattering, filling gutters

Creeks carrying brilliant floating colors
Into swirling oblivion

Cold, freezing rain pelting leaves
Left behind,

Autumn's art work is complete.

B.B.

Some Fifties Facts

I want to include a few facts about the fifties before I go on to junior high in 1957.

When I was born, Harry Truman was president. Next there was Dwight Eisenhower. People wore buttons with his *I LIKE IKE* campaign slogan. Ike was responsible for inserting *Under God* into the Pledge of Allegiance. I have always respected him for that. He did not care for cats and I once read that he ordered all cats found around the White House to be shot. I did *not* respect him for that!

Davy Crockett enjoyed a wave of popularity when I was in elementary school. It started with a song about him, and then, it seemed everything had an emblem of Davy on it. I had a Davy Crockett ballpoint pen and two T-shirts with his image.

Most children watched *The Howdy Doody Show* on Saturday mornings, and the *Mickey Mouse Club* was on in the afternoons.

TV dinners came out and were supposedly named because people could heat them up and enjoy eating in front of the television.

Play-dough was a hit with children. *Pop Beads* were just plain fun. You could wear a strand, take them off, and *pop* them apart, bead by bead. Then you popped them back together. They came in a variety of colors, including pearl.

McDonald's opened its doors in 1955, but it was several years getting to our area. Rock and Roll had its roots in the fifties and caught on quickly. Everyone loved *Elvis.* I watched his first TV appearance on the *Ed Sullivan Show.*

People gave themselves home perms. One of the most popular brands was a *Lilt.* The one for children was called a *Toni.*

Barboursville Schools 1957 – 1963

Junior High

At Barboursville Junior High, I took art from Miss Alice Wilson, and loved it. She worked especially hard with students who showed an interest, and I was one of them. We worked with clay and did a craft or two. Mostly, I drew and painted. She let us work at our own pace.

We had a long lunch hour. My two friends and I always went across the street for lunch. We also had time to look around in the ten cent store or even go to the public library. Most of the schools are now located out of town or have a closed campus and students cannot leave.

While I was in junior high, hula hoops came on the scene. Rock and Roll was going strong, and I was the first to show up at school wearing *Tan Shoes with Pink Shoe Laces,* a popular song by recording artist, Dodie Stevens. I bought one new 45 speed record each week to play on my portable RCA record player. I glued pictures of "Fabian" to the inside.

High School

Barboursville High School was a new experience. My distant cousin, who went to school with me at Watson in third grade and moved away, was once again my good friend. We shared a locker and one of our textbooks, as teachers were short on this particular one. We were not in the same classes, so it worked out. We stuck funny notes in the book to each other. It was hard not to laugh sometimes when opening the book and finding a silly note. We ate lunch each day at *Pirates Corner.* It wasn't cool to eat in the cafeteria. I must say, I was sick of hot dogs long before I finished my three years in high school. That was all they made up ahead, and if we wanted anything else, it took most of our lunch period and left no time to hang out with friends. So, we had hot dogs.

After school, most teenagers went home and turned on Dick Clark's *American Bandstand.* I knew the names of most of the kids on *Bandstand* who showed up each day to dance. The Philadelphia teen stars made frequent appearances on the show. They included: Frankie Avalon, Paul Anka, Fabian, and others. *Motown* groups were popular as well. Some of the songs of that year were:

Kathy's Clown—Everly Brothers
I'm Sorry—Brenda Lee
Save the Last Dance for Me—The Drifters
Running Bear—Johnny Preston
The Twist—Chubby Checker
It's Now or Never—Elvis Presley

Art continued to be the subject I loved. I had won my first drawing contest in fourth grade, sponsored by a local TV show, and I won several more after that. I had Libby Caligan for tenth grade art. She was to become my supervisor when I began teaching art many years later. She was a no-nonsense teacher and stood up to two senior boys on the first day when they wandered into the room to cause trouble. They towered over her, but she went right up and pointed her red-nailed finger at them and said, "Get out of my class *now,* and don't come back." They left, fast!

In my junior and senior years, I had a handsome young art teacher by the name of Vernon Howell. He had a record player in the room and had all the popular records of that time. I remember the Fleetwoods, *Come Softly to Me, and Night Train* going through my mind as I worked. Transistor radios had come out, and I had one. We could play those as well. I looked forward to his class and the assignments every day. Mr. Howell remains an outstanding artist today, winning many awards and honors for his work.

I also met my future husband this (junior) year. His name was Jim and he was a freshman at Marshall University. I met him through my girlfriend who was dating a friend of Jim's. We had so much fun going roller skating that first time. We continued to see each other on dates, playing miniature golf, going to movies at the East Drive-In Theater, or sometimes the Tri-State Theater in Ohio. In the summer, four of us would spend the day at Dreamland Pool. Once we went to a far-away pool called "Rock Lake."

Some of the popular songs during my junior year were:

Telstar—The Tornados
Peppermint Twist—Joey Dee and the Starliters
Do You Love Me (Now that I can Dance)—Contours
Stand By Me—Ben E. King
Runaway—Del Shannon
Return to Sender—Elvis Presley

When I was a senior, my sister Dodie gave birth to a beautiful baby girl that she named Cela. I was seventeen, the same age as Dodie was when I was born. I was in study hall that morning and her husband's youngest brother was in the same study hall. I went over to him and said "Did you know Dova and Cecil have a new baby girl?" He grinned and said, "Well, I'll be-dogged!" Dova and Cecil moved with the baby and their son, who was twelve or thirteen at the time, just up the road on Cyrus Creek, into a new brick home he had built. Years later, Dodie's husband was in charge of the brickwork on Huntington High School, Cabell Midland, and many, many other schools and buildings.

Some popular songs from my senior year were:

Rhythm of the Rain—Cascades
Louie-Louie—Kingsmen
Surf City—Jan and Dean
Then He Kissed Me—The Crystals
Sugar Shack—The Fireballs
I Will Follow Him—Little Peggy March

My Marriage

I have always loved the *golden oldies* of my teen years. They bring back so many memories. One that brings back fond memories is "Theme from a Summer Place." After seeing *A Summer Place* with Sandra Dee and Troy Donahue one summer at the drive-in, Jim proposed to me. We decided to keep our engagement a secret for a while. He gave me a beautiful engagement ring with a three-fourth carat diamond on Christmas.

I attended a business college in Huntington. Mother thought I should become a secretary because they made good money. Although I did well in school, my heart was never in it.

Jim and I were married by the Baptist minister of Cyrus Creek Baptist Church in the summer of 1964. We did not have a big wedding—that was not for me. I did not want an audience while making such life-changing vows. We went to Black Water Falls for a short honeymoon. Later, I began working as a clerk-typist for an insurance company in Huntington.

Losing Pop October 13, 1965

Our dead are never dead to us, until we have forgotten them.
George Eliot

Jim and I had been married a little more than a year when my grandfather, Lewis Brillie Scarberry, died. More than two days before, after the family doctor told us there was no hope for recovery, the family had been awaiting his death. Six months before this fatal stroke, my grandfather's left leg had to be amputated just above the knee. The doctor thought he had made a remarkable recovery for a man his age, which was eighty-six.

I did not want to go to the funeral home to face the reality of Pop's death. I felt obligated to go anyway. People commented as they always did on how *natural* he looked. When I looked at him, I could see nothing natural about him. He looked dead, lying there with his hands folded on his chest, surrounded by a solid wall of flower baskets. I would rather have remembered him the way he *was*. Pop, the only grandfather I had ever known, was gone, and now there would be no more ghost stories.

Financial Challenges

Time goes on, and after two years of living in a small apartment, we had a house built on a lot beside my parents. We lived in the basement for nearly a year before we were financially able to have the house built on top. My brother-in-law, Cecil, bricked it. We chose an orange color brick, and it was an attractive little house. A few years later, he built us a nice brick fireplace in the basement. He would not charge us anything for this job. He loved my pecan pie, and told me to just make him a pie. What a good deal—I made him two pies!

We had our first child before our third anniversary, a beautiful little boy. My middle sister, Emalene, gave me a baby shower. She adored little Jimmy and often said she could just take him and raise him as her own, as she had three girls and only one boy.

I had quit my job with the insurance agency to stay home with my son. Our *first financial challenge* happened when he was nearly three years old. Jim worked in the lab at Goodyear Chemical. He belonged to the union and they could not come to an agreement for a new contract after the old one had expired. So they stopped work and carried signs, known as a *strike.* For work, Jim signed up with Manpower. This was a temporary job agency that called people for jobs of short duration. He worked several jobs, then Emalene's husband was doing an addition to their home and he hired Jim to help with it. After that was complete, Dodie's husband put him to work mixing mortar for a church he was bricking. Jim also took his turn walking picket. He received a small check for that. There was never a lazy bone in my husband's body, and he did all the work he could get and kept our bills paid. We never took any government handouts or even considered it.

When an agreement for a contract was reached, Jim had been off work for three months. Our son had turned three years, and I went to work in the Barboursville Library. My mother consented to babysit, and I paid her a small sum each payday. My job did not pay much.

The *second financial challenge* came as another plant strike when our daughter was just an infant. Jim began almost immediately working with a crew building Linmont Apartments in Barboursville. He gained valuable building experience from this. He is a quick learner and this job kept him employed up until the strike ended. It had lasted six long months! Once again, we weathered the challenge and Jim kept our bills all paid. We had only spent money on necessities.

Jim went back to work at the plant, and after a few years, he was offered a position as lab supervisor. The only problem for him was that it was a salaried job (or non-union), and he was not sure he wanted to work without the union's support. We talked it over and I convinced him he would be fine without the union. If he did not take this position, we would only have more strikes to deal with each time a contract expired, and two long ones like we had lived through were enough! He became a lab supervisor and was never sorry.

The blessing from the last strike was that Jim had learned so much about construction, he built a house as an investment for his uncle. He did this on his off days, and since he worked swing shift, he put in hours between shifts and whenever he could. This house sold and he built another one for his uncle.

Our family was complete and we were doing well, but I began to feel something was missing. I had continued doing art for the library (posters, banners, bookmarks, brochures) after our daughter was born, but I regretted not having a college degree. I wanted to do more with my art, and earn more money for our children's education.

I told Jim my feelings and we decided that after our daughter was potty-trained, I would enroll part-time at Marshall University and work toward a degree in art education. Best of all, as a teacher, I would have the same hours as my children and be home with them during the summer. I would get to stay in the field I loved. My parents would watch the children when Jim was working. I applied at Marshall University and was accepted!

Marshall Student 1974

College was a challenge, but being older was definitely an advantage. I knew my purpose for being there and did my best in every class. Younger students skipped class or left early, and I knew it was immaturity on their part, and many were wasting their parents' money. I had to make every dollar count. Instead of rushing out to buy every item on a studio art class list, I took note of what I already had at home. Some supplies listed were never used, so I did not buy them. I sold my textbooks as soon as I took my finals and put the money aside to help pay next semester's tuition. I rented a parking space and since I was a Tues/Thurs student, rented it to a Mon/Wed student. This paid for my spot. So I went to M.U. and took care of my family on what my husband earned, without any student loans.

I loved the art studio classes, but did as much of my work as possible at home. I had to take care of my children. I would give them clay to work with while I was doing a ceramic project on the kitchen table, or let them paint with their watercolors while I did mine. They both loved doing art with their mom. Once, I took my daughter, Beth, with me to Lake Vesuvius for a day of painting with my watercolor class. She took her little kit and painted, too.

English composition classes were great. I did well in those as well as American literature and creative writing. Education classes went very well, too. The only class that worried me was *zoology,* so I put off taking that course as long as possible. I knew they dissected gross things in lab, and I could never do that. As it worked out, I had a nice lab partner and told him I would fill out both our lab manuals if he would dissect for me. The professor never objected (I don't think he even noticed). A day was coming up when *each* of us was supposed to dissect a sheep eyeball, and I was worried. Just the thought of it made my stomach churn. My son, Jimmy, who was twelve, happened to be out of school for Veteran's Day. He said, "Let me go with you

Mom. I'll dissect that eyeball for you." It worked fine, and that's how I made it through zoology!

While I was in college, a whole new world opened up; the world of the *other arts.* As a student, I could get tickets that permitted me to attend entertainment events free. I went to ballets and was spellbound by the beauty of movement. I attended theater plays and thought how much I would love painting the backdrops, or scenery. I went to concerts that introduced me to so many kinds of music, through the M.U. Artist Series. I learned from and enjoyed so many things I had never had access to while growing up in a rural area.

THE BALLERINA

Slender dancer,
Butterfly on wing,
Your movement
Defies gravity.

Satin toes,
Dandelion seed
Caught in a soft breeze,
Hummingbird
Of a thousand dances.

B.B.

THE BALLERINA, II

Swirling, twirling,
Flashes of brilliant color
Suspended in mid-air.

Leaping, pirouetting,
Elegance in motion,
Bending gracefully.

Folding slowly,
Head downcast in closing,
Her dance, complete.

B.B.

Graduation, May 1980

After five and a half years, I graduated *magna cum laude* from Marshall University with an AB degree in art education. What an accomplishment for a mother with two children! I was so happy I made it and thought about Miss Harrison, my fourth grade teacher. I hoped I would live up to her prediction and make a *fine* art teacher. I was hired as an art teacher in Cabell County.

We outgrew our home on Cyrus Creek. We had two children, a dog, a cat, two goats, and two cars with only a one car garage. We tried looking for property to build in the same area, but there was none for sale at that time. Jim bought acreage at Ona from his uncle. He used his skills in construction to build our dream home. It was two stories with both an upstairs and a downstairs porch. I had a large art studio to work in, in one wing of the house. The style was *Southern Colonial.*

Jim built a barn on the hill behind our house for goats and one horse. The property had huge boulders for the goats to climb on and we had a big hay field at the top of the hill. We bought the thirty acres adjoining our property.

Loss 1985 and 1989

My dad's health had not been good for about the last two years. He suffered some light heart attacks. After surgery for the removal of an abdominal tumor, his heart could not take the strain and he passed away. I had been driving my parents around and helping out for some time, and now I continued to do my best to help Mother. She was afraid to live alone. I quickly furnished my fourth bedroom with new furniture for her. She could stay with us anytime she wanted. We included her on outings with the children. She had always loved them dearly.

Time passed, I continued teaching, and Mother seemed to have more and more health problems. I did all that I could for her, as she had no energy. Eventually, she had surgery. She never recovered, and passed away after being in the hospital more than a month. She had lived a little more than four years after Daddy died. It was so hard to go on without my mother to talk to, and take her places, and call on the phone. We were always close. I found myself talking to her as I drove. I could almost see her beside me in the car. I just could not get over the fact that she was really gone. One night, three months after her death, I was having a scrambled type of dream (like we all sometimes have), when it appeared a curtain opened. There stood my mother wearing a pink dress, her favorite color. She was wearing her usual make-up—pink lipstick, and blusher, with her hair styled pretty. I said "Mother, do you know how long I've been waiting to hear from you?" She replied, "Oh, Brennie, it's so peaceful here. I'm real happy."(This was the way she talked, using "real" instead of "really.") I started to speak to her again, but woke up instead. I tried and tried to go back to sleep and re-capture my mother, but she was gone again. *I know in my heart she came back to me in that vision to let me know she was fine and to help me let go of her.*

My sister, Rosa, and I have shared many losses through the years: the loss of our grandparents, our parents, our three older sisters, as well as aunts and uncles. I believe these losses have brought us closer. She lives out of state with her husband, but we visit each other every year, often more than once. I don't know what we would have done without each other for support.

SOLACE

The peace of the woods
Overwhelms my racing thoughts
Slowing them to the pace
Of the box turtle
Confidently making his way
To an unknown destination.

The serenity of watching
A family of squirrels
Playing and chattering
Gathering and storing next
Winter's supply of walnuts,
Calms my tortured heart.

The coolness of the moss
And newly spored ferns
Clinging to the jutting
Mammoth boulders
Refreshes my soul
With hope anew.
B.B.

Written upon the death of my mother, Gladys Peyton Edwards, July 4, 1989

THE HOUSE

The little frame house
Stands abandoned, silent
Listening for the sounds
That used to be:
The rocking chairs squeaking
In unison on the front porch,
Heavy padded footsteps
Hurrying to the door,
The ringing of the phone,
A "clink" as ice fills a glass.

The little frame house
Stands and waits
For the annual fresh coat of paint,
The cleaning of rain gutters,
The sound of a lawn mower as it
Makes its way around the
Brilliant colored summer flowers.

The buzzing of the car ignition
As the "Duster" is started
And taken for its daily short trip
Out to the store.

The little frame house is sad,
My heart is heavy.

Those things that once
Had little meaning
Are etched in my memory
Like golden treasures
And taken out daily
To savor.
Mother and Daddy, how I wish
You were here.
B.B.

Written one year after my mother's death, July, 1990

My Teaching Years

As a teacher, I taught art in four elementary schools, on a cart in all of them, going room to room. This went on for three years before I was finally given a room in one of the big schools. It was less tiring after this. I went home and worked some more. Friday evenings after school, I went to the grocery store for a week's supply of food. Then I went home and prepared dinner. All day Saturday, every week, I cleaned house between loads of laundry. Sunday was my day to rest, after church. Thank God! I mean that. God knew what He was doing when He made Sunday the day of rest! I taught elementary art for fourteen years.

I finally decided to try middle school. The good thing about students this age is they can clean up after themselves. Little children, especially lower grades, do not. In middle school, this took some of the work load off my shoulders.

After my third year of teaching middle school art, a mammogram showed I had a small tumor. Biopsy revealed it was the dreaded *BC*. It was so unexpected, I was stunned. How could this happen? What had I done to cause this? Was I going to die? All these things went through my mind, and I now understand that it is very common to feel this way.

The first step was to have surgery. I was able to have a lumpectomy, which is the removal of the very small tumor, in my case. My husband was with me all the way. I went home with a tube under my arm to drain the fluids. This had to be taken care of and emptied daily. Jim did this task for me, knowing how squeamish I have always been. Then there were the treatments. Jim was right there holding my hand during all four treatments. My appetite was gone. A person's appetite becomes very strange and things I had always loved now made me nauseated. I lost weight because of this, but I did very well with the chemotherapy, and my blood count came right back to where it should be. I then had radiation treatments.

All my treatments, including chemo, had taken a total of five months. I was finished. Time passed, and my check-ups were always good. It has been fourteen years since my hard fought battle with BC. I seldom think of it anymore, and I was reluctant to even mention it in my book. However, it is part of my life, and if it gives even one person hope and courage to fight breast cancer, then it has been worth mentioning. The things that kept me going were faith in God, a positive attitude, good doctors, prayers, and a good husband for support. I also had a wonderful friend and former counselor, Harriet, who encouraged me all the way. She had been through it herself. Having breast cancer was the biggest physical challenge I have ever encountered. God let me win.

For nearly nineteen years I taught art full-time in Cabell County. I have taught an additional eight years as a substitute teacher after retirement. I had many very memorable students through the years and truly hope that I taught some to enjoy doing art and maybe encouraged others to continue with their art education. I sometimes look at a few pieces of art I have saved from my students, and wonder what they are doing now.

My own children grew up and graduated from high school. Each of them graduated from Marshall University without student loans—that was important to me. My son earned his degree in art education and then his master's degree in *printmaking.* He teaches art in a high school. My daughter earned her degree in journalism. She has a position where she uses her talent as a writer. She is also artistically talented.

Jim and I had an empty nest. We decided to *down-size.* It meant leaving the community where he grew up, as well as good neighbors and most of his family. Since we had lived on Cyrus Creek for seventeen years, Jim did not mind moving me back to my *roots.* We bought a lot, built a new house and moved back to *Cyrus Creek,* back *home.*

Front Porch Thoughts

Today, as I sit on the front porch of my home on Cyrus Creek, the sun is shining again and the spring rain has stopped. A double rainbow beautifies the sky over the hills in front of me. The forsythia is in its yellow splendor. I can see the slight greenish cast to the trees, getting ready to put out new leaves. Soon the wisteria will be in bloom again. I have some growing on a fence in my front yard. Jim started it two years ago, knowing how much I love it. At the bottom of the road, leading up to my house, the trees become heavy with purple wisteria blooms in spring. After this, the locust trees put out their long clusters of white blooms. I love to put down my car window as I drive through, to sniff the delicate fragrances.

I regret not having tulips, lilies, and some of the other spring flowers in my yard, but our wildlife critters think these flowers are for snacks. The lilac bushes are growing and the irises, my favorite, are left alone. Lavender is budding around the old tree stump. When it blooms, the bees work constantly over it. It smells wonderful and I often tie up little bunches to hang in the house. It is also great to put into glycerin soap that I make with my granddaughter, Dhania.

Our home is on a wooded double lot. The squirrels and chipmunks come every day to the feeders, along with our chickadees and cardinals. A little tufted titmouse lands on the edge of the seed can every morning as Jim goes out to feed. It never seems to be afraid of him. In the evenings, the raccoons come for their evening meal of dog food and whatever goodies we have left over. They sometimes fight over a piece of cake or pie. Last summer, a mother raccoon brought her five babies to the feeders in the daytime. They came every day for two or more weeks. This meant refilling feeders after the squirrels had eaten. Occasionally there is a 'possum and twice we have seen red foxes. The deer come to the salt lick often and bring their young ones. Wild turkeys come and scratch through the seed that drops to the ground.

We watch these little critters through our kitchen window while we have breakfast. I love them all; such wonderful wildlife to enjoy! God is good and I am so thankful every day for all He has given us. Most of all, I am thankful to be home again—on Cyrus Creek, where my memories for the love of my family have led me for the second time.

CATS

Animals are such agreeable friends

--They ask no questions,

--They pass no criticism.

G. Eliot

A Note to my Readers

While reading *Front Porch Sketches,* you learned about the kittens I had as a child. There were five of them through the years. They were my playmates and companions and such a good part of childhood. I promised *more about cats later.*

There were four more cats in my adult life. They were all so unique in their own way. I wrote about each of them. They were: *Teka, a seal point Siamese, Lady Clarissa; a solid white Turkish angora, Marissa; a white copper-eyed Persian; and Susie; a small cream Persian.*

These special little friends have all crossed over the *Rainbow Bridge* and I will never forget them. Lady Clarissa was a one-woman cat and was the one most sensitive to my feelings.

I have started with a true story about Teka, then Lady Clarissa, and finally, Marissa and Susie. The last two were with me together. They were eight months apart in age.

Teka's Missing Kittens

For a second anniversary gift, my husband gave me a beautiful seal point Siamese kitten. I named her "Teka," and soon got into the habit of taking her with me in the car wherever I went, rather than leaving her at home to get into mischief.

Teka came to love riding in the car, and she often jumped through the open car windows of anyone visiting us and waited for a ride.

By the time Teka was a year old, I had a new baby boy to care for. Not having as much time to spend with her, and fearing she was keeping him awake with her loud meowing, I moved her outside to her own little house in the backyard, complete with her name over the door and a brick patio. Shortly after this move, Teka became pregnant. She gave birth to four beautiful multi-colored kittens. She was a protective mother, seldom leaving them except to eat or jump viciously onto the back of any unsuspecting dog that wandered into our yard. She would send it yelping in pained surprise!

Early one morning, when the kittens were five days old, I was awakened by Teka's loud, hoarse meow. I jumped out of bed and went to see what her call of distress was about. To my utter astonishment, the kittens were not in her house! I knew that mother cats often moved their babies, but I could not imagine where they were and why Teka was not with them. She was still looking at me and meowing in that bewildered voice, refusing even to sniff the breakfast I offered her.

"Teka," I said, "don't tell me you moved the kittens and forgot where you put them. I'll just have to help you look."

Together we covered every possible hidey-hole in the yard, and then searched my mother's yard and out-building next door. No kittens.

After puzzling over the kittens' disappearance for the better part of the day and watching Teka's repeated march from our yard to my parents' yard, it finally hit me—only one thing could have happened to those kittens.

When my father pulled into the driveway that evening, I was waiting anxiously. He looked startled as I ran and jerked open the doors of his car almost before he had stopped. There, in the rear floor of the car, behind the driver's seat, were four meowing, hungry kittens, crawling blindly (their eyes were still closed) over each other in search of their mama.

Teka, loving to ride in a car as she did, had wanted her family to share her love for riding. She had placed them, one by one, in my father's car. He had driven off before she could join them. He did not know they were in the car with him until Teka and I found them that evening. By some miracle, he had left the front car windows half-open and this was the only reason the kittens had survived the heat on that summer day.

This true story happened more than forty years ago. We remember Teka as the most unusual cat we ever owned. I hope she is in cat heaven, riding in a car with her whiskers blowing in the wind!

Portrait of a Friend

A beautiful, loyal friend came to share our home many years ago when she was about one year old. When I saw her for the first time, the name "Clarissa" came to mind. I cannot imagine any other name that would be appropriate for such a feminine, elegant cat.

Clarissa had just given birth to a litter of three kittens. The owner, who had not had her very long, wanted a new home for her. I took her.

Typical of the Turkish angora, Clarissa had a long, graceful body, a small head, very petite pink nose, clear blue eyes and long, silky white fur. The texture of the fur on her belly was the most delightful down softness imaginable. She wore a pink collar with a jingle bell, which she would deliberately jingle if she was in the mood.

Clarissa learned that there was a chair and a wicker basket bed with a soft pillow she could occupy anytime. Clarissa quickly chose me as her mistress, over everyone else in my household. Indeed, we did seem to have a rapport unshared by anyone else. She loved to curl up on my lap and purr contentedly while I watched my favorite soap, "All My Children." But first, she would ask for permission with a tiny meow.

After Clarissa was spayed, she quickly recovered and became even more of a "person's cat" than a "cat's cat." She never wrapped around my legs to cause a fall, nor wandered far from the door when allowed outside, unless I went for a walk with her. She was considerate, just as any friend should be.

Don't get the idea that my little friend was perfect. She had a panic attack when we moved to our new home at Ona. She hid behind a large sheet of cardboard in my art studio for three days.

Gradually, she came out to explore her new surroundings. She cautiously checked out every room, downstairs, then upstairs. When I heard her galloping at play like a small pony on the new stairs, I knew she had accepted her new home.

One Saturday morning my son locked Clarissa in the art studio at 5:30 AM to stop her demand for breakfast at such an ungodly hour. Not being used to such degrading treatment, she retaliated by using the floor instead of her litter box. When Jimmy opened the door to free her, she stalked out with her ears laid back, tail high in the air, and fire in her normally cool eyes. When he tried to pet her, she nipped at his hand with a look that said "How dare you!" She followed me around all morning with funny little meows, describing the inhumanity of my son. I agreed, and assured her with a cuddle that "mean ol' Jimmy" would never shut her up again.

Clarissa had a sixth sense that told her when I was going on a trip, although I never went often. The evening I packed my suitcase for a trip to Boston, she followed at my heels. When I stopped, she stopped, and stared me straight in the eye, as if to ask, "Are you leaving me?" When I returned, four days later, she was the first to greet me the minute I opened the door. After a hug, she proudly followed me around, digging her claws into the carpet, making a sound like Velcro as she pulled them out.

When I was worried or ill, Clarissa knew. She brought comfort with a lick of pink sandpaper on my hand, by curling in my lap, or cuddling snugly against my back in bed. If I were too hyper or nervous to sit down, she would follow me, mimicking my restlessness.

At Christmas, the tree became a huge exotic toy for Clarissa. It bounced back and forth from her antics with the ornaments, and she sometimes tangled herself in the tinsel. She always found a new place to sleep on a gift-wrapped box for the duration of the holidays. There were always two or three packages for her.

My little friend eventually crossed the rainbow bridge after being my best friend for sixteen years. I enjoyed this marvelous little creature as a companion and a friend. Clarissa was gentleness, serenity, independence, and grace.

Cat People

A number of years ago, I made a discovery about "cat people." Introverts choose cats for companions, while extroverts choose dogs. Of course, there are exceptions. Introverted people love the independent nature and aloofness of the cat. They are very much alike and can develop great respect and compatibility together. For example, they respect one another's space and moods.

When there is more than one cat in a household, there usually is a dominant one, often the one who came first. This is sometimes referred to as the *pecking order* in the animal world. After Clarissa, my husband gave me a lovely white Persian kitten. I named her "Marissa." Eight months later, he gave me sweet "Susie." She was a little fluff of cream Persian, with huge copper eyes. It was amusing to watch as they gradually became acquainted. I worried that Marissa would harm little Susie, as she wanted to smack her and constantly chase her around the dining room table. I stopped worrying when one chase ended with Susie chasing Marissa.

Marissa often resented attention given to Susie. For example, if I spent more time than usual on Susie's daily brushing, Marissa would come over to "help" by washing Susie's ears. Then, washing would turn into bites. I was not usually aware of what was happening until Susie jumped up and ran away. Marissa would repeat this if Susie was first to curl up with me at bedtime. She wanted to be there first, and then she would usually accept Susie's presence at the foot of the bed, but never in *her* place.

Cats all have different, very individual personalities, just as people do. Marissa and Susie could not have been more different. Marissa was affectionate and loved being picked up and told how beautiful she was. I could tell by the smug look on her face that she understood exactly what I said to her. She was alert, dignified, and always crossed her front legs when reclining. Susie, on the other hand, did not tolerate being picked up, but loved being stroked and told how beautiful *she* was. She always sat up like a panda bear in a chair and slept on her back with paws in the air. She was like a comic little monkey. I respected her space and seldom picked her up, unless for a good reason.

One rule people should know is to never laugh at a cat if she does something clumsy. She will be humiliated, for she considers herself the perfect example of gracefulness. I nearly broke this unwritten rule once when Marissa was in a wild, playful mood one day. Running and chasing, she leaped onto the TV, which had a VCR on top. She landed on this slippery surface and scooted off, falling behind the TV, which was turned across a corner. She did not have the space to jump out, and failed on two escape attempts. I moved the TV to allow her to come out on her own. She sauntered out, cool and nonchalant, while I ran to the bathroom, closed the door and laughed until tears coursed down my face! She never knew about this.

In summary, if you are an introvert, cats would most likely be your ideal friends and companions. They usually come litter-trained, don't mind staying alone while you are at work, and they don't have to be walked. They are agile, graceful, and loyal in a way many "dog people" cannot understand. It does not take long for them to own *you*. They are almost like people, except they are purr-fect!

I lost my last little Persian, Susie, nearly six years after we moved back to Cyrus Creek. She was twenty years and five months old. No cat could ever replace her. When the time is right, I will have another cat, with a different "purr-sonality" to love.

THE QUIET

She tiptoes about

On little pink pads

And sits staring me
Eye to eye
On quiet haunches.

Accepting that I
Have nothing to tell,
Gives a farewell meow
And moves on.

B.B.

TO MARISSA

You are so elegant with
A coat of luxury white,
The automatic crossing of
Your front legs
Shows such breeding and poise!

Your senses are sharp, alert
Your ancestors' hunting instinct
So apparent in your crouch,
As you watch your birds.
The affection you show me
Is dignified and real,
Our favorite time is bedtime
When you snuggle close
To my side and purr.

Good Night, Pouf-Pouf.

Written March 23, 1993

Beloved Persian cat, my friend
September 20, 1990—Sept 24, 2002
B.B.

TO SUSIE

One of a kind, that's
What you are,
Little monkey on your back
In a chair.

Sitting upright in Dad's chair,
You seem to say, "It's mine,"
And it is, for you melt
Our hearts with your
Funny, endearing ways.

Sweet little fuzz-ball, your
Bird watching is just a hobby,
As you fall asleep with your
Little forehead against
The window.

Your "catch me" game is so
Much fun as we play
The game and laugh!

I love your little fuzzy heart,
Sweet Susie.

Dear little Persian friend
April 21, 1991—September 7, 2011
B.B.